The Positivity Pulse

Transforming Your Workplace

www.thepositivitypulse.com
Blog Us at www.positivitypulse.com

Book Cover Design: Kristin Requena,
GetGraphic www.getgraphic.net
Illustrator: Brenda Brown,
www.webtoon.com

ISBN: 145642517X
ISBN-13: 9781456425173

This book is a home run for managers and their direct reports! . . .Hard-nosed managers could learn a lot from this simple message. Bravo Sherry!

Vice President, Wall Street Investment Banking Firm

This book not only epitomizes what Sherry believes in but how Sherry runs an organization. As a long time employee, I have been provided the opportunity to see the Positivity Pulse in action and the many benefits that come from it. As an employee, you feel valued, respected and appreciated. It is a pleasure working in a company that believes and "lives" this philosophy. This is a must read from employee to CEO!

Connie Masullo, Systems Performance Specialist

I've had the honor to work with Sherry Blair for six years now. I sought her out while working for another employer because I was looking to feel connected to my agency and valued as an employee. I also had a desire to learn and grow as a professional, and Sherry and her agency embodied many of the values that I was looking for at that time. Sherry is extremely passionate about her work, and she is one of the most compassionate leaders I've ever met. She leads from her heart, and her leadership style provides the type of work environment that attracts people to her and her agency. Sherry is constantly looking for new and improved ways to support, guide, and build inner wealth in her employees (and everyone she meets), and The Positivity Pulse provides the precision tools for accomplishing this goal.

ToniAnne Lofrano, Events Coordinator

In the past decade of working under the leadership of Sherry Blair she has been an outstanding mentor to me and a shining example of what a leader should be so much so that she has inspired me to pursue a career in the helping profession. I admire her dedication to her profession, her passion to do a good job, and her understanding and care for people in and out of the office. From the first time I met her, I noticed she was a natural at engaging people and finding the positivity in those around her.

Brendaly Sanchez, Employee Relations Specialist

The Positivity Pulse takes you on a powerful, inspiring, and motivational journey to a brighter, more successful self and workplace. It provides the tools required to nurture, develop, and become successful, efficient, and vibrant employees!

Ashley SanGiacomo, Care Manager

What a timely message!
As global consciousness progresses from independence to interdependence, every relationship that we have, especially with our colleagues, who we spend increasing amounts of time with in this daunting economy, impacts every other relationship, including the relationship we have with ourselves.

I could easily identify Justice and Moody in my corporate world, and now I feel I am armed with the tools to change them and myself to be more like Senora Corazon.

If more people read and applied the nurtured heart approach at all levels within the organization, we could all be singing "Shiny Happy People" by R.E.M..."Put it in your heart, where tomorrow shines, gold and silver shine..."

Narisha Maduray, Business Intelligence Specialist

The Positivity Pulse is a must read for anyone in a leadership position. Leading from the heart will transform your workplace, leading to a truly peaceful environment where employees will flourish and feel truly appreciated!

Sherry Blair captures the essence of true leadership with her creative writing style and practical examples of leading from the heart. Nurtured Heart combined with Positive Psychology principles leave the reader motivated to make immediate change! This book will change the status quo of all leaders forever!

Debbie Riddle, LCSW, Executive Director, Total Family Solutions

The most valuable resource any organization has is their workers. Frontline workers represent the face of any organization and can make or break your efforts to promote the mission of your organization. *The Positivity Pulse* outlines a plan of action to assist any organization in achieving the best from each worker. This book is a transformational work that allows the reader to understand how to focus on the positive actions each individual makes and to recognize and utilize teachable moments to increase a worker's motivation for becoming their most efficient self. *The Positivity Pulse* makes the transformation of any workplace an achievable goal by making each step real to the reader. It is the tools that *The Positivity Pulse* outlines that makes this book a must for anyone manager who is looking to get the best from each employee. Understanding how individuals embrace change and an outline of very specific tools allows any organization to begin to make the changes necessary to transform into a positive working environment which in turns allows the organization to maximizes its resources and provide the highest quality output. I recommend this book to anyone who is interested in becoming the best manager, coach, mentor, and boss. It is well written and incredibly thought provoking!

Elizabeth E. Manley, CEO, Caring Partners, Inc.

Sherry Blair has written an insightful, witty and very useful manual on how to transform any workplace into a more positive, productive, heart centered environment. By seamlessly and very informatively integrating leading corporate motivational ideologies with the powerful ancient wisdom of the Nurtured Heart Approach, Ms. Blair presents a clear, tangible road map for Success. As a manager and clinician I have been inspired and rejuvenated by this book.

Joe Clem LMFT

Preface

Howard Glasser

Howard Glasser (New York University, 1974) is the Executive Director of the Children's Success Foundation in Tucson, Arizona. He is designer of The Nurtured Heart Approach and the author of Transforming the Difficult Child, published in 1999 and currently the top selling book on the subject of ADHD, and several other books on his approach. He lectures internationally, teaching therapists, educators and parents about The Nurtured Heart Approach, which is now being used in hundreds of thousands of homes and classrooms around the world. Howard is former director and clinical supervisor of Center for the Difficult Child and he has been a consultant for numerous psychiatric, judicial and educational programs.

Sherry Blair has a most impressive curriculum vita. She's a graduate of Columbia University and holds a dual Master of Science in Social Work with concentrations in Policy Analysis and International Social Welfare and Industrial and Organizational Psychology. She is a licensed Clinical Social Worker, a Board Certified Professional Counselor as well as a Professional Coach.

She uses all of this academic knowledge to provide organizational consulting, coaching, behavioral health services, training and education across several counties in New Jersey. In a typical workweek, Sherry might do in-home counseling with an intensely troubled child or teenager and his family, give a seminar on Positive Psychology or the Nurtured Heart Approach, or consult with a major corporation – all while juggling the responsibilities of running her own business. Her role encompasses leadership, quality assurance, marketing, program development, clinical work (as a therapist to children, families and adults), business and executive coaching, employee assistance services and critical incident debriefings. And she's found time, while keeping all of these aspects of her work life thriving, to write this – her first book.

Sherry has long been invested in using and teaching the tenets of Positive Psychology, which led her to the Nurtured Heart Approach - an approach I developed in the 1990s for transforming difficult children into their inherent greatness. She began using the approach in 2008 and became an Advanced Trainer of the approach in 2010 and has applied the approach with her trademark intelligence, wisdom and enthusiasm to her work as a counselor, supervisor and consultant. In this book, she demonstrates the utility of this approach in the corporate world, and she does so brilliantly.

When I first taught the Nurtured Heart Approach to parents who were learning to transform their challenging children, I was struck by how often people brought me stories about the ways in which its principles became useful – even transformational – in their workplaces:

- One parent who had a large car dealership went on and on about the changes the approach had inspired for him at work. He had changed the way he interacted with his employees, and this had created a new blend of leadership that he loved and that had made his staff much more happy and productive.

- A principal of a school went on and on about how teacher attrition had come to a screeching halt. The previous pattern of teachers calling in sick on Fridays and Mondays was no longer an issue. Her teachers had come to live the vision that had originally brought them to the field of education.

- The head of a large public works department and parent of a difficult teen attended a four-week parenting class where he learned the Nurtured Heart Approach. In weeks following, he shared that treating his workers and management according to the tenets and techniques of this approach had transformed his department from top to bottom. These formerly disgruntled workers, who often had to toil for long days in the hot Arizona sun, were seeing things differently due to relationships that were now radically positive.

- In the clinic that I personally directed for years, everyone there already knew the approach. They knew I was using the approach in my capacity as an employer and supervisor. Despite this transparency, we all marveled at how the approach impacted our ability to function incredibly well as a clinic and as a team. This improved the services we performed and benefited the families we served.

Although I've seen the potential benefit of this approach in workplace settings for years, I also knew as clear as day that I would never, ever be the person who took the Nurtured Heart Approach to businesses and corporations at any large scale. My passion has been and remains bringing the approach to children, parents and educators.

So: I could not be more thrilled that the great Sherry Blair has emerged into this realm of exploration marked by the emergence of this wonderful book and a growing stream of transformed workplaces.

I'm especially impressed and honored by Sherry's leap of faith in adapting this body of work that is not yet (but that is on its way to being) evidence-based, despite her dedication to the empirical path she's been a part of as an academic scholar. The Nurtured Heart Approach resonated with her at a level that has clearly compelled her soul, and she's run with it. With beautiful stories and characters, she crafts a wonderful depiction of how this method born out of work with challenging kids is a natural fit in the world of work. She brings clarity about how a more nurturing and heart-full workplace can help rather than hinder the bottom line. In my humble opinion, this is the way in which businesses can explode into further iterations of success, accomplishment and greatness as we move forward into the second decade of this new millennium.

Sherry's rare combination of qualities of greatness – her great compassion, enthusiasm, drive, commitment, empathy, heart, awareness, vision – shine through every page of this book. I am so appreciative of her deftness in bringing the approach that came through me out into the corporate world.

To Sherry's greatness - and to yours!

The Positivity Pulse

Transforming Your Workplace

By Sherry A. Blair

with Melissa Lynn Block

Table of Contents

Leading from the Heart

When you are tuned into your heart,
your Inner Wisdom…
then your energy lightens up and your vibration literally changes.
You become a beacon of light and peace.
You become an uplifter and a peacemaker.
–Christiane Northrup, MD

Fortune 500 companies have widely used Ken Blanchard's *One-Minute Manager* series to improve performance. Spencer Johnson's *Who Moved My Cheese?* and John Kotter's *Our Iceberg Is Melting* are other best sellers that have helped millions to lead and collaborate in the corporate world. The work of all three of these authors has inspired countless organizations and individuals to improve leadership skills and adapt to change.

In their Situational Leadership model, Blanchard and Hersey demonstrate the need for leaders to understand employees from a developmental perspective in order to support them in their various workplace responsibilities. A developmental approach enables leaders to effectively support employees through directing, coaching, supporting, and delegating. Johnson and Kotter write about how individuals can come together to solve problems and adapt to change. Each author's work is, in its own way, about creating relationships that motivate, unite, and set the stage for achievement.

While they emphasize the importance of relationship—Blanchard's stance that leaders act as supportive coaches to team members, for example—there's room for more explicit means to optimize relationships in the workplace.

But something's missing from the work of these authors: a *precise set of tools for building and supporting relationships.*

In the #1 bestseller *Who Moved My Cheese?* we are introduced to the book's four characters—two mice and two "little people" (mouse-sized human beings) who live in a maze. Their supply of cheese has disappeared. The mice, Sniff and Scurry, have the confidence in themselves to make the changes necessary to survive and reach the goal held by all four characters, which is to find a reliable new supply of cheese. But Hem and Haw are reluctant. They get stuck in many ways. In the end, they find a new cheese supply as well, but they travel weakly along the trajectory of change, and they suffer many more setbacks and disappointments. (The term *languishing,* as used in this context, is the opposite of flourishing. Work done in this area by psychology professor Barbara Fredrickson is addressed in more detail in chapter two.)

They are languishing, unlike their constituents—who possess an "inner wealth" that helps them flourish.

Let's imagine this story a little differently. What if these four characters had been able to communicate and relate in a way that brought them all to the new cheese together as a team, with no one left behind and no one having to weaken along the way? How might these characters work more effectively as a team? How might this improve productivity and enhance the company's bottom line? What might help them establish relationships that would better enable them to grow, change, and achieve together?

When we don't have good relationships with ourselves, it's much more difficult for us to relate to others well. If Hem and Haw had learned how to develop character strengths and virtues (or, as I'll refer to it later, *inner wealth*) and positive emotions, they might have navigated their difficulties in a very different way—more like their rodent counterparts, Sniff and Scurry. How might these characters transform their own relationships with *themselves* in ways that make them better able to relate in a positive, constructive way with others?

Let's look at the message of Kotter's change management book to see how these missing relationship tools might have changed the story.

Our Iceberg Is Melting is the tale of a group of emperor penguins who discover that the iceberg they call home is disappearing into the ocean. One penguin, Fred, isn't a part of the colony's leadership council, but he makes the best decisions about what to do and whom to ask to join his team. Most of the other penguins become plagued with worries and doubts that create misery, but Fred has the courage, wisdom, and confidence to approach the leaders with the ideas that ultimately save the colony. Increasing positive relationships from the frontline penguins to the Leadership Council and every penguin would enhance the interrelatedness of this penguin colony—a group that desperately requires collaborative efforts to survive, grow, and change.

If these penguins could learn to divert their attention away from useless worries, resentments, and doubts—instead, making a conscious choice to remain in a positive, confident state of mind that cultivates success and harmony—**they would learn to bypass blaming, judging, and negative thinking**. Instead, they would choose to see and reflect the greatness inherent in themselves and in their fellow penguins.

With this kind of transformation, the story would lose much of its drama, but it'd be much better for the penguins!

In the tradition of Kotter's penguins and Blanchard's mice and little people, we'll begin with an illustrative tale—this one, about caterpillars and butterflies...

Chapter 1

Creative Recognitions, Inc.

Just when the caterpillar thought the world was over, it became a butterfly.

–Proverb

In a gorgeous green meadow dotted with wildflowers, the frontline staff of Creative Recognitions, Inc., is hard at work. Their mission: to train corporate leaders in the latest and most effective styles of leadership. At the offices, frontline workers handle scheduling, paperwork, and correspondence. Leadership creates and gives trainings, keeps up to date on the latest in corporate leadership, and manages frontline workers.

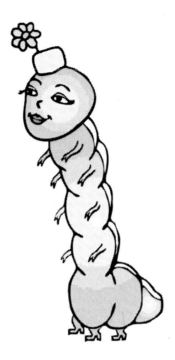

Upon first entering the offices of Creative Recognitions, Inc., one sees the smiling face of Isabella. She is flourishing in her job. Coming to work is a joy; she feels supported and appreciated. Work is a place she can grow and change in a positive way. Even as a frontline worker, she understands that the role she fills is just as important as that of the company's CEO. Sure, she makes mistakes and breaks rules, but there's no fallout and no drama. Mistakes are no big deal. She doesn't dwell on what she's done wrong. Instead, she quickly steps back into her greatness.

To be continuously bathed in positive feedback, all Isabella needs to do is make her best effort to keep up with her work, follow the rules, and adhere to policy. No wonder she wants to shine! As she continues through her day and works on her project, she turns more and more golden. The silk strands of her chrysalis are beginning to form. She's well on her way to metamorphosis.

This is Justice. When he makes the effort to do well, he goes through his day hearing comments such as "Thanks!" or "Good job," but he never quite knows why he's being thanked or how he's doing a good job. At the end of each day, he feels as though he's had nothing but junk food to eat—he's had plenty of seemingly positive reinforcement, but he craves more. He never quite feels satiated.

On the other hand, even for smaller infractions of policy or rules, he is given lots of negative attention. Sometimes the higher-ups even call a big meeting to discuss his rule-breaking. Justice feels picked on by his supervisors. Although getting in trouble feels terrible, Justice feels drawn to breaking rules, or to walking that fine line between rules followed and rules broken. It's the only way he gets the attention he craves from leadership and from his front-line peers.

Justice has very few gold stripes on his body, and he hasn't figured out how to begin wrapping himself in the comforting softness of silk. He becomes fearful that he won't make his deadlines. If this happens, he won't be able to move into the next phase of the project.

Sometimes Justice wonders why he even bothers to come to work. He works just as hard as Isabella and his accomplishments are similar to hers, but for some reason she is changing and growing, moving at an astonishingly rapid pace toward project completion—toward metamorphosis. It even seems that she is more liked than Justice. "It's just not *fair*," Justice grumbles.

Isabella and Justice's fellow frontline workers each fall into one or the other category: progressing toward metamorphosis or stuck in a state of inertia; feeling recognized for even their small successes or as though they can't do anything right; growing and changing rapidly or wanting to metamorphose but not knowing how to begin.

What makes some of these workers grow and flourish while others languish? These differences have a lot to do with the leaders who guide and supervise their work. Ultimately, the responsibility of the company's leadership teams is to guide team members toward the chrysalis stage, even as they themselves accrue golden stripes and build their own chrysalises. Leaders need to fill frontline workers to capacity with the nutrients they require to transform in the final stage, where project completion—metamorphosis—can take place.

Some leadership teams are having greater success with this than others.

Team Chrysalis

Mr. Moody, Mrs. Crabtree, and Mr. Silencio, who supervise Justice and others like him, are members of Team Chrysalis. These leaders have diverse qualities and strengths. Some are new team players and some are seasoned. Their gold stripes are well established and their silk chrysalides are taking shape, but each is stuck in a unique way. Each encounters different kinds of obstacles to imparting their wisdom and greatness to the people in their lives.

Mr. Moody is a seasoned member of this team. He's close to retirement and has contributed in magnificent ways to the company's sustainable development. Although he regularly thanks his team members and frontline workers for doing a good job, his moods can sometimes make him difficult to get along with. He himself has lots of gold stripes, but for some reason he seems stuck—he has not moved far enough into his own transformation to set a truly inspiring example for Justice, Isabella, and their co-workers.

Mrs. Crabtree is task oriented and full of wisdom. But in her role as a team leader, she seems to spend much of the day barking orders and punishing her staff. She has a tendency to lecture when someone does something wrong. Even on a good day, she's abrupt and a bit crabby; she's in a constant state of frustration because she sees around her only employees who are making mistakes! She can't seem to escalate disciplinary actions far enough to have an impact. At the same time, she doesn't ever seem to notice when her fellow team members or frontline workers are shining.

"That's just what I expect from them," she'd likely say if someone asked her why she never gave positive feedback to her team. "They're going to have to do a lot better than this to get a pat on the back from me. Besides, they get a paycheck to do what they were hired to do."

In private moments, Mrs. Crabtree feels unhappy that her gold stripes are barely showing and that her chrysalis is tattered and in need of much more silk before she can enter her own metamorphosis. Like Mr. Moody, she knows that she isn't setting a great example for her fellow leaders or for the followers who count on her for guidance—but she doesn't know how to change to set this example.

Mr. Silencio is the quiet type, but his contributions to the team are nothing less than stellar. He has many gold stripes and has finished his chrysalis in preparation for metamorphosis, but he has not yet begun his transformation in earnest. Although frontline workers and fellow team members learn a great deal from his intellect, he says barely a word to them directly.

Whether they're doing well (which gives him a good feeling) or breaking the rules (which bothers him), he says nothing. His frontline workers have no trouble getting away with rule-breaking when he is around. On the other hand, they don't feel inspired to do a better job, because Mr. Silencio doesn't seem to have a preference or a voice one way or the other. He is stuck in his own chrysalis.

The Nurtured Heart Warriors Team

Mr. Kodak, Mrs. Polaroid, and Ms. Canon, members of the Nurtured Heart Warriors Team, believe that creating a brilliant workplace is all about celebrating what's going well. They do not agree with top-down leadership styles, choosing instead to value the voice of every single person who works for the company. Their mission is to nurture personal and professional development—to support everyone into their metamorphosis to greatness. Their transformation into butterflies is complete, and they're ready to show others the way.

This is Mr. Kodak. He seems to notice everything that's going right. Whomever he speaks to comes away feeling special. Even if it's something small—a choice to follow the rules, or just showing up and paying attention—he has something good to say about it. Practically everywhere he goes, Mr. Kodak takes "snapshots" of successes, both miniscule and massive, and he's unfailingly generous when giving feedback to team members about those successes.

This is Mrs. Polaroid. As a more seasoned manager, she can keep up with Mr. Kodak in terms of noticing and acknowledging success. Like a Polaroid camera, she captures successes as they happen, then deepens that image of success by clearly stating how those successes reveal strengths and virtues. Her unique, intense style takes some getting used to, but in the end, this ability to hone in on what's going right—and on what's so right about it—makes her an invaluable member of the management team.

Ms. Canon is the team's ultimate policy implementer and relentless rule follower, but she's not one to lecture, reprimand, or scold when rules are broken. Instead, she recognizes *rule-following*. She keeps the team in full compliance by offering frequent reminders to those staying on task: *you are wonderful for* not *breaking rules and for following policy*. Ms. Canon appreciates team members for their willingness to change old habits, for staying in healthy control and for re-routing themselves back to compliance when they break rules or fail to comply with company policies and procedures. She's firm and strict, but also compassionate, loving, and proactive.

Señora Corazon: CEO

Señora Corazon, CEO of Creative Recognitions, Inc., has been accused of wearing rose-colored glasses. She seems to believe, sometimes beyond reason, that all people can flourish. Her view is that giving recognition for every success, brilliance, and accomplishment is good for everyone, including the one who gives that recognition. She loves to notice what people are doing in the moment—or even what they're wearing!—and to take time to tell them what she's observing. She communicates to her people that she values them for positive attitude and great work ethic.

Even when staff members seem to be having a rough day, she finds ways to positively acknowledge them for their ability to deal with hard times or difficult tasks. Other leaders have not agreed with her approach. They stand behind traditional ways of ruling over workers with enforced disciplinary action. This doesn't feel right to Señora Corazon.

Señora Corazon is especially magnificent at bringing frontline workers back to balance when necessary. While she doesn't always hit the mark, she responds to her own errors and negative thoughts by redirecting her focus to what's great and right in the moment. Like the Nurtured Heart Warriors Team, Señora Corazon has blossomed into a brilliant butterfly—but she's the most brilliant of them all.

Imagine It...

Let's pause for a moment. Please indulge me! Stop and take a deep breath. Imagine how magnificent it would feel to be wrapped in gold and silk. Embrace and savor this vision in your heart. Who wouldn't shine when bathed in gold and supported by the strength and softness of silk—when bathed in recognition and appreciation?

Continue to breathe this in as you read on.

Why Caterpillars and Butterflies?

Anyone who watches a caterpillar for any length of time knows that its main driving force in life is its appetite. It has an intense need to obtain as much nourishment as possible to prepare for transformation. Caterpillars eat constantly—and they can't eat just anything. Each breed of caterpillar needs a different food in abundance in order to change and grow into a magnificent butterfly.

> There is nothing in a caterpillar that tells us it's going to be a butterfly.
>
> —*Buckminster Fuller (1895–1983), inventor and architect*

Similarly, we human beings require a huge amount of nutrition to grow and transform—but not the caloric kind (most of us get too much of that). We thrive most when we receive abundant spiritual and psychological nutrition in the form of *Our appetites for this kind of positive relationship exist just as much in the workplace as they do in any other realm of life.* love and positive relationship—just like the relationships cultivated between the Nurtured Heart Warriors team and Isabella.

In preparation for metamorphosis, the caterpillar weaves a silken chrysalis—a word derived from the Greek word for gold. It demonstrates that while change is inevitable, it doesn't have to be painful. For us humans, positive relationship helps us to relax into transformation. It gives us the hope, faith, and sense of self-worth we require to keep morphing into greater and greater versions of ourselves. And this is what makes a workplace really golden: employees who already see themselves as successful and who genuinely want to build further success.

Butterflies are regarded as symbols of peace, happiness, and fidelity. In various cultures, butterflies have been symbolic of resurrection, the soul, eternal life, young love, transition, lightness, and beauty. They have been called "flowers that fly." In central Asia, Aztec Mexico, New Zealand, and Zaire, as well as in Christian mythology, the butterfly is considered a symbol of the soul. In Greek myth, Psyche (the Greek word for "soul") is symbolized by a butterfly. Ancient Christian tombs often included a depiction of a butterfly; Christ has been illustrated holding a butterfly in many works of art.

The caterpillar unquestioningly enters into transformation. Her body and her environment change in shocking ways as she follows her destiny. The butterfly's transformation is a fitting symbol for the life journey of the human being. Hopefully, the twists, turns, setbacks, and successes we experience all contribute to morphing us into what symbolism writer Avia Venefica calls "ever-finer beings."

As she goes into the dark night of metamorphosis to emerge completely transformed, she exemplifies trust and hope—a model for transformation for those who are held back from becoming their greatest selves by fear or uncertainty.

As our caterpillar selves transform into butterfly selves we realize that, contrary to what Buckminster Fuller said about caterpillars and butterflies, our butterfly selves—our qualities of greatness—were in us all along. That butterfly-ness was in our DNA just as butterfly-ness is in the DNA of the caterpillar. The metamorphosis is just about changing the expression of what we have always possessed.

And so the story goes…

Monday Morning

Isabella is due into work at 9:00 a.m. She arrives around 8:45 a.m. As she passes the coffee room, Ms. Canon—who is filling her cup—says brightly,

"Good morning, Isabella! I see that you're here early. We cannot thank you enough for getting to work on time and for not being late! What a great role model to the rest of our team. Thank you for that!" Isabella begins her day feeling golden.

Justice arrives shortly after Isabella—at 8:50. He's very conscientious about time. Usually, he arrives early enough at work to take care of any personal needs before diving into work promptly at 9:00. While walking into the building, he passes by his supervisor, Mr. Silencio—who barely acknowledges his existence, giving little more than a brief, unsmiling glance. Justice starts out his day with low energy.

Shortly into what appears to be a hectic Monday morning, Isabella is at her desk, managing a multitude of tasks. While passing by, Mr. Kodak says, "Good morning, Isabella. I notice how you're multitasking and getting so much accomplished! Quite impressive!"

Isabella thinks to herself what great bosses she has and how fortunate she is to have them. She feels a sense of connectedness deep within herself and a confidence regarding her work performance. As Isabella is nourished by her bosses, she begins to grow more golden stripes, taking on a burnished golden glow. She feels herself brimming over with creative ideas for completing the team's new project, and she can't wait to get started on the next phase.

On the other side of the office, Mr. Moody notices Justice working feverishly at his desk. "Good job, Justice!" he says as he walks by. Justice pauses for a moment. While it feels good to be told he's doing a good job, he wonders: *What am I doing well, exactly?* Although he's grateful not to have been the target of one of Mr. Moody's legendary bad-mood-induced jabs, he doesn't feel like he has been nourished by what has been said to him. Justice considers following Mr. Moody to ask him what exactly he has been doing right, but quickly changes his mind. Mr. Moody is not particularly approachable. Sometimes, when Justice asks for guidance, assistance, or support, he is met—often, without warning—with one of Mr. Moody's marvelous moods. Brushing off his thoughts, Justice goes back to his work. There is no luster in his being. His gold stripes are barely visible.

As it gets closer to lunch hour, Mrs. Polaroid approaches Isabella to discuss the arrangements for the afternoon meeting with the CEO, Señora Corazon. Isabella is more than well prepared. She has achieved her goal of having everything organized and confirmed prior to taking her lunch break. Impressed, Mrs. Polaroid happily tells Isabella, "You are so incredibly organized, Isabella! I notice how hard you are always working. This shows us what a team player you are. You're demonstrating valuable leadership skills. Thank you for all you do for us!"

Isabella is more lustrous than ever. Her golden stripes grow exponentially; she shines with radiance.

Conversely, Justice begins to move at a snail's pace. When he's not completely unfocused, he wonders why he is at this job. Sometimes he feels invisible. He is falling behind on some of his deadlines and is quickly becoming more and more distracted. He wonders what his girlfriend is doing and decides to send her a text. She texts back right away. Back and forth the texts fly. This is not the first time that Justice has broken the rule of not using his personal cell phone in the workplace, but when Mr. Silencio walks by and notices him doing this, he doesn't say anything. Then, he's also caught by Mr. Moody, who calls him out. "It's just a quick message," Justice tells him. "Oh, OK. No problem," Mr. Moody replies, and keeps walking.

And then, Mrs. Crabtree catches him texting. The subsequent lecture goes on and on and on: "How many times do we need to remind you, Justice, that the use of personal cell phones is not permitted on the company's time? I cannot understand why this is so challenging for you! As it is, I can clearly see that you've fallen behind for our deadline for this afternoon's meeting with Señora Corazon. I am sorry, Justice, but we are going to have to have a discussion about this *right now*! Let's go into my office to discuss this matter. And we also have to call Human Resources. I just cannot believe we have to address this again and again, Justice. When will it end? Now I have to spend all this time with you because you insist on using your cell phone to conduct personal business at work!" Even as Mrs. Crabtree waxes poetic about Justice's misdeeds, Justice barely hears a word of it.

After Mrs. Crabtree has finished with him, Justice slithers back into his cubicle. He feels like an empty shell. His faint gold stripes are quickly disappearing. He longs for 5:00 p.m. to arrive. Maybe he could go home sick? Yes—he could tell Mrs. Crabtree that he was trying to get his girlfriend to make him a doctor's appointment because he hasn't been feeling well. He could make up a story and just go home early.

Wait, he thinks. *If I go home now, I'll never make that deadline. I've got to get back to work. And it's only Monday.* Deflated, faded, he turns back to his work.

At lunch, Justice and Isabella sit down in the break room. Justice briefly greets Isabella, but he doesn't feel like chatting because he feels jealousy toward her. She looks radiant. Her excitement about her current project,

Project Transformation, is palpable. She can barely contain her enthusiasm; clearly, she's yearning to get back to work as soon as she finishes her lunch.

Justice has really enjoyed working with Isabella and respects her a great deal. They've had a close collegial relationship. But today, he's in no mood for all her joy and positive energy. In fact, he's in no mood to be around anyone. Isabella asks him what's wrong.

"I got in trouble for texting with my girlfriend," he tells her. "Mrs. Crabtree brought me into her office and yelled at me for a good ten minutes. I was in such a bad mood, I almost faked being sick so I could go home."

"But you decided to stay and keep working," Isabella tells him brightly. "That's real commitment. That's perseverance."

Unmoved by Isabella's positivity—really, he's only half listening—Justice says, "I guess I got what I deserved." He finishes his lunch and trudges back to his desk. Maybe he isn't physically sick, but he's sick internally. He's leaking energy, and he can't figure out how to shake this feeling of being disconnected from his co-workers and bosses.

Nourishment for Transformation

Children and adolescents develop in stages; so do employees, teams, and students. Employees go through stages of development in the workplace. Some research posits that it takes a new employee six months to acclimate and assimilate in his or her new environment. Consider the more seasoned employees along a trajectory—a golden path—that also requires ongoing nutrition to support flourishing mind, body, and spirit.

Theoretically, from the day a person steps foot into your workplace, he or she is beginning in the earliest stages of development in your organization. With each new employee, you have a golden opportunity to nourish him or her with all of the nutrients required for positive growth and change.

When we notice, in detail, what staff or students do right, we are supporting their metamorphosis—their transformation into a human being who is flourishing rather than enduring.

Most of us don't see the caterpillar as stunning or graceful. But in essence, the caterpillar is the spirit form of the butterfly. Only if that spirit is nurtured during the caterpillar stage can it transform and grace us with its intricacy, brilliance, and beauty.

Butterflies, once transformed, require continued nourishment to flourish. Many prefer the sweet taste of nectar. And all staff, even executive team members, need continuous nourishment. They too thrive better when the nutrition offered is sweet (like the nutrition Isabella receives) rather than bitter (like the nutrition Justice received from Mrs. Crabtree).

At Creative Recognitions, Inc., transformation occurs when recognition and appreciation are offered instead of negativity. This likely makes intuitive sense to you. It points the way down a road that an employee like Justice feels compelled to follow, to the consternation of those who wish he'd make different choices.

Negativity doesn't get us what we want as leaders. Even when it does, the rewards tend to be short-lived and to create problems that have to be dealt with later: contentious relationships, hurt feelings, and choices to go against policy or procedure. Staff best develop toward success when they are "fed" with detailed positive feedback.

Most of us get that a positive road is better for all, but few know how to achieve a consistent flow of honest, heartfelt, positive recognition and appreciation—the psychological and spiritual nutrition that best supports employees in being the best they can be.

When the caterpillar cannot access the nutrients it requires to transform, it slows down and gets stuck in that stage. Lack of positive relationship can cause us to become downtrodden, depressed, doubtful, worried, angry, or isolated.

Your most important role as a leader is to provide nourishment at every level of the workplace. When that role is fulfilled, employees thrive and the entire organization flourishes. Problems are dealt with promptly and efficiently, and the next step is back into greatness.

Positive recognitions are energizing. Negativity saps energy, but it also has a way of energizing the recipient to make more negative choices.

Administratively and organizationally, this kind of environment increases productivity, creates positive workplaces, and energizes brilliance and teamwork. Employees feel valued. They want to come to work and do their absolute best.

Human beings can get stuck too when forced to do without positive social, emotional, and intellectual interrelationships.

In a sense, you're also the mother butterfly (even if you're the wrong gender for motherhood, you can still play this symbolic role) who has found the ideal place for her caterpillars to flourish, enabling them to do so rather independently. Once you have placed those caterpillars just so and given them high-quality nutrition for a while, they become more able to flourish and transform on their own.

Now, let's head back to Creative Recognitions, Inc., in time for an important meeting...

PROJECT TRANSFORMATION MEETING: Monday, 2:00 p.m.

LOCATION: Main Conference Room

This pulse of positivity works best when balanced with a kind of "tough love" where noncompliance, conflicts, and negative energy are addressed head on with total consistency.

Señora Corazon waits patiently for her management teams and their team members to join her in the main conference room. As she waits, she thinks: *Project Transformation is crucial to the on-going development of the company. In today's market, having the ability to be dynamic and to change with the many challenges with which we are faced gives us an edge. It's what keeps our company in business.* She sets her intention to observe, in her teams, whose dynamism and flexibility seem to be coming through strongly and whose seem to be flagging. She wants to discover what makes the difference between employees who are energized and flourishing and those who are disengaged, discontented, and languishing.

As everyone arrives, she immediately observes that members of the Nurtured Heart Warriors team—both frontline and management—are bursting with ideas. They seem genuinely happy to see one another. Frontline workers are even happy to see their team leaders, Mr. Kodak, Mrs. Polaroid, and Ms. Canon. Señora Corazon feels the pleasure of watching them interact with one another with mutual respect. In the chatter before the meeting begins, these team members engage in a reciprocal exchange where they are all learning, growing, and transforming.

As the other team members convene, Señora Corazon notices an astonishing disparity. Members of Team Chrysalis sit quietly and seem disengaged. "These meetings are such a waste of time," one team member mutters.

As he hurries in from his desk, Justice notices how Isabella and her team members all have a golden, glowing look. He wonders why his team members are so dull and negative. He thinks that the other team must have a secret weapon—something that is uniting them in fast, joyful movement toward project completion.

Señora Corazon sees this polarity of negativity and positivity. In her mind, she mounts a critical analysis of what is happening under her leadership: *Half of my employees are spilling over with abundant intellect and energy and amazing ideas. Half of them are presenting brilliantly and transforming right before my eyes. Others are observably downtrodden, sullen, disengaged, and even angry. Some seem very connected to each other; others seem disenfranchised.*

Señora Corazon is certain of one thing: that all of her managers and team members are amazing. She wouldn't trade in a single one. Some are shining, while others are stuck, unable to transform. Project Transformation will not work for their company if only half of the employees make it.

As she starts the meeting, Señora Corazon notices how the members of Team Chrysalis respond as she begins to do what comes naturally to her: recognizing her employees' outstanding contribution in active, experiential, and proactive ways. She notices how Justice instantly begins to glimmer when she notices him making a real effort to stay focused in the meeting. She knows Justice had a challenge with this. She says, "I need everyone to bring all of their attention and energy to every meeting. Justice is setting the example today—he's completely focused, keeping his eyes on me as I present to you all. Thank you, Justice!"

The leaders of Team Chrysalis respond with warmth when their CEO makes a point of acknowledging their successes in detail—even when those successes are small ones. Even when they're just doing what they're supposed to be doing, this visionary CEO sees that they could be making other choices to do what they *aren't* supposed to be doing, and calls them on their good choices out loud where everyone can hear.

It quickly becomes clear that the pulse of positivity has remarkable effects—not only on those who had thus far been steeped in negativity, but also on team members who were already thriving. Señora Corazon herself feels the benefit of modeling positivity, and when the meeting adjourns, everyone's in high spirits. They return to their work with renewed enthusiasm. Everyone's just a little more golden.

"Time to find a way to bring this pulse of positivity into our whole workplace," Señora Corazon muses to her assistant in the meeting's aftermath.

"Hmm. I like the sound of that," her assistant answers. "The Positivity Pulse!"

"Yes!" Señora Corazon says with characteristic passion. "Commence Operation Positivity Pulse!"

The Positivity Pulse Begins to Beat!

Señora Corazon realizes that she has the responsibility and the power to change things for employees who have felt detached, disaffected, and steeped in negativity. She also sees that the transformation she wants to make in her own workplace will bring great clarity to the work her company does to help others transform their workplaces.

First, she decides to spend several days simply noticing what is happening under her leadership. Sometimes, worried and doubtful thoughts come up. *Can I really transform my workplace? Can I really create this vision I imagine where positivity is the common denominator to all we do? What if I fail?* She finds, however, that by quickly "resetting" herself back to the project of getting this Positivity Pulse to work in her organization, she finds herself right back in the flow of her intensity, from which she can move forth with zeal and passion.

Over the next two days, she commits herself to assessing the pulse in her company. She notices the different styles of her six managers from the Nurtured Heart Warriors Team and Team Chrysalis.

Mr. Kodak, Mrs. Polaroid, and Ms. Canon are often heard relating to their team members. They are all working and producing, but their relationships stand out as most meaningful. An outsider coming into their work space is likely to want to join them. When conflict comes up, they unceremoniously address it and work through it swiftly. These managers relate to one another in a manner that feels like a celebration.

Conversely, Team Chrysalis is leaking energy. They barely relate to one another unless something goes wrong. The frontline workers are visibly deflated. Mr. Moody, Mrs. Crabtree, and Mr. Silencio collectively have an apparent and resounding *negative* pulse! Clearly, this management team does not seem to notice the greatness of their team members—or even the greatness they themselves possess. But Señora Corazon finds that if she walks through their work station and notices Justice or the others in positive ways, they respond with golden brilliance.

Señora Corazon notices how the positivity and collegiality evident between leaders of the Nurtured Heart Warriors team seems to be completely missing from Team Chrysalis. Team leaders seem constantly stressed, even frenzied. They bark orders and struggle and push to meet deadlines.

There's no doubt in Senora Corazon's mind that Team Chrysalis managers require an entire makeover. Their negative energy is leaking onto their frontline workers. She knows that Mr. Moody, Mrs. Crabtree, and Mr. Silencio are all capable and have great hearts. With a few tools, she reasons, they'll be able to shift from negativity to positivity, which will enable them to manage their staff more effectively—to nurture their greatness. And to determine what those tools would be, she could use the approach of the Nurtured Heart Warriors Team.

Señora Corazon also realizes that she will have to fearlessly, relentlessly model this approach herself. She knows that if she copies Mr. Kodak, Mrs. Polaroid, and Ms. Canon precisely, Project Transformation will be a smashing success that will take her company to a new level of greatness.

Although she is naturally in alignment with the Nurtured Heart Team's approach, she has to be honest and evaluate herself in this process. She too has to make some changes. She's fantastic at creatively recognizing everyone and at maintaining order and compliance, but she also sees that Team Chrysalis remains stuck. She'll have to kick it up a few notches by amplifying her recognitions and appreciation.

She gathers her management teams together for an urgent meeting. Once everyone has arrived, she tells them: "All of you know that the Nurtured Heart Team is closer to metamorphosis than Team Chrysalis. If we are all going to come together to complete Project Transformation on time, some of us will need to change our ways. Starting now, we're all going to learn from the Nurtured Heart Team about how we can relate to one another more effectively and with greater positivity. We're going to bring their Positivity Pulse to our entire organization."

At first, protests erupt from Team Chrysalis. There are excuses; there's finger-pointing and blaming. But Señora Corazon holds fast to both her edict and her positivity. Refusing to give the negativity any energy, she simply says, "This is how things are going to be. You can deviate from the plan if you want, but your performance evaluations will be negatively affected by that choice."

Eventually, everyone gets on board—some less willingly than others. Over time, both leadership teams observe and imitate the ways in which the Nurtured Heart Warriors Team communicates and leads. They even spend one-on-one time with these leaders to find out more about their *internal* dialogues—how they talk to and nurture themselves. As Team Chrysalis begins to play around with these new tools, workers like Justice begin to enjoy coming to work. They start to see that they are valued and that they have much to offer. They begin to pick up the very tools their supervisors are learning. Creative Recognitions, Inc., is transformed.

Chapter 2

The Heart-Centered Way

In times of prosperity, you can sleep your whole life through, imagining that God's [1] responsibility is just to keep the party going with all possible kinds of party favors. Faced with real danger, however, such smugness, entitlement, and complacency have no hope of surviving. You come to the end of the fantasy that the Divine is there to give you what you want. Slowly, painfully, but with more and more authentic hope and authentic joy, you start to suspect that we are here not to bask in God's love, but— willingly, freely, and with answering love—to give all we have to Love's work of transformation so Love can transform all we have, all we are, to gold.

–Andrew Harvey, *The Hope: A Guide to Sacred Activism*

Transforming Leadership: Servant Leaders, Leading with Love

In my expansive work in industrial and organizational psychology, I've seen many calls to a specific paradigm shift in the workplace. The call: to shift away

---

1   Please feel free to substitute another name for the "higher power" referred to by Harvey as God: Oneness, the Universe, good orderly direction…

from top-down, autocratic styles of leading into modes that are more about service and leadership from the heart. Positive psychology, including the creation of positive institutions, as well as transformational leadership and servant leadership are important elements in this shift.

Kevin and Jackie Freiberg's book *GUTS: Companies that Blow the Doors off Business-as-Usual* (Random House, 2004) gives substantial evidence in support of "leading with love," tapping into the wisdom of the heart to make leadership decisions and create relationship with colleagues.

Business leader Jackie Freiberg calls upon us to "lead with love"; management guru Kenneth Blanchard describes the journey of life as moving "from a self-serving heart to a serving heart."

The Freibergs give examples of Fortune 500 companies whose gutsy leaders are willing to lead with love, including Southwest Airlines. These companies demonstrate that this type of leadership is not just good for employee morale and smooth, efficient company operations—it's also good for the bottom line:

> In some circles, love is considered unbusinesslike—an amorphous concept that may be appropriate only in the professional lives of nurses, physicians, social workers, and teachers. Clearly, in this view, love doesn't belong in a big brawny business. We disagree. Inherent in the human condition is the need to be loved, to be cared for, and why would we think that need evaporates when we enter the workplace? In fact, it doesn't make sense to expect your employees to function effectively in an environment that doesn't acknowledge their psychological or emotional needs. (p. 157)

In my own work as the founder of my company and as a consultant who coaches organizations to enhance team performance, train managers, and optimize team cohesiveness and communication, I have found an approach that works powerfully to bring a heart-centered relationship into the workplace. It is an ideal complement to leadership models that have inspired thousands of companies around the world. It provides an answer to the question: **If better relationships are key to success in the workplace, how, then, can those relationships be consciously created?** This approach creates a culture of greatness and abundance where everyone flourishes.

The relationships my clients have with one another are almost always founded in caring, but when they learn this set of precision tools, their ability to nurture each other toward success improves exponentially. **Leaders learn to lead from their hearts, in synergy with their minds.** They increase their teams' sense of connectivity and relatedness to one another, which accelerates the functionality of those teams. When a more precise tool for creating positive, mutually enriching relationships is added into this mix, everyone benefits.

The Heart and Spirit of Change: Examples of Heart-Centered Leadership

When love and skill work together, expect miracles. –John Ruskin

Shelly Lazarus, chairperson and CEO of the advertising firm Ogilvy & Mather, convinced IBM to consolidate what had been a scattered ad campaign into a unified brand. This decision brought $750 million in billings to her firm that year—nearly doubling earnings compared to those brought in the first year that IBM was a client. Lazarus' company is also behind the historic Dove campaign featuring women of all shapes, ages, and sizes as beautiful in their own right. As one of the 50 Most Powerful Women in Business, Shelly Lazarus believes that both customers and employees need to feel engaged for a business to succeed. In her book *Why the Best Man for the Job Is a Woman: the Unique Female Qualities of Leadership* (Harper Business, 2001), Esther Wachs Book quotes Lazarus:

> I start from a point of view that says to lead people, they must be engaged. One way to engage them is to issue orders, make demands, and frighten people. To me, that does not get you the best results.

Few would argue that this less beneficial leadership style could come from leaders' hearts. The alternative, of course, is the kind of leadership advocated by Dr. Kenneth Blanchard (who calls himself Chief Spiritual Officer of his company), one of the top ten leadership giants in 2010 and ranked third in a thirty-leader roster of top management leaders worldwide. Dr. Blanchard speaks passionately of what he calls *heart leadership*. He teaches that positively relating to and serving employees is what makes the difference. In Blanchard and Zigarmi's third book of the *One Minute Manager* series, Blanchard's approach is described as "the heart of management." In *The Servant Leader: Transforming Your Heart, Head, Hands & Habits*, Blanchard and Hodges challenge us: are we *self-serving* leaders, or are we *servant* leaders? They posit that the servant leader can lead more effectively.

Great Leadership Begins with Great Love

When looking at the way industry has evolved and how it has shaped our behavior in the workplace, we can easily see how we have evolved to being somewhat distant and disconnected as leaders. In Blanchard's work, we are called upon to bring out the greatness in every person with whom we come in contact. This is an imperative described in many of the world's great spiritual traditions.

A groundswell of spirituality and positivity is rising in Western culture. We are becoming aware that there is a more satisfying, less destructive way to be in this world and with each other. That something's missing in a life ruled by what's wrong with ourselves; that a life ruled by judgment and mean-spirited competition is incomplete and unnecessary.

As we integrate the call to greatness into corporate life, **we lead the way in creating a legacy that preserves the human spirit not only in the workplace but overall.**

Although many of us don't yet see the beauty of the heart-centered way, a part of us knows that we are asleep to what is truly possible in human relationship and in humanity's legacy on the planet. We can be generous, compassionate and positive rather than stingy, cutthroat and negative. We can choose to see more of what's right and complain less about what's wrong. And we're all better off every time anyone decides to make that shift—even if it isn't us. What's true of the transformation of humanity outside the workplace needs to make its way into the workplace.

That operating from a foundation of love just makes more sense than operating from a foundation of fear and anger.

The Nurtured Heart Approach—the End of "Business as Usual"

Decision makers in the workplace serve as gatekeepers who can choose to direct staff, students, management teams, and organizations into a more positive, heart-centered way of being. We are responsible for building inner wealth in our workplaces—for taking the initiative to move away from "business as usual." In the end, this is a choice that every person gets to make in every waking moment of every day.

Will my next encounter with another person or with myself be positive or negative? What will I choose to

Indeed, to fail to engender a spirit of positivity and heart-centered relationship in the workplace is counterintuitive and counterproductive.

observe, comment on, praise, or criticize? No matter how good our intentions, it can be difficult to make the conscious choice to be positive in one's

There's an old Cherokee teaching story where an elder tells his grandson, "Within all people, a battle goes on between two wolves. One is negativity—anger, sadness, stress, contempt, disgust, fear, embarrassment, guilt, shame, and hate. The other is positivity: joy, gratitude, serenity, interest, hope, pride, amusement, inspiration, awe, and—above all—love." The grandson asks, "Which wolf wins?" and the old Cherokee replies, "The one you feed."

observations and interactions without appropriate tools. This chapter introduces a set of relationship tools that serve this purpose beautifully: the Nurtured Heart Approach.

The Nurtured Heart Approach is a model for interacting with others and with ourselves in ways that support this transition. It works in any relationship dynamic—parent/child, teacher/student, manager/employee, therapist/client, spouse/spouse, friend/friend— to build positive percep-

tions and language. It can positively transform a whole organizational culture, one relationship at a time.

The Nurtured Heart Approach Story

This approach is a revolutionary set of tools for communication and relationship that nurtures individual confidence and motivation and creates much more rewarding relationships.

The Nurtured Heart Approach was created by psychotherapist Howard Glasser. While working as a family therapist, Glasser found that his efforts to help difficult children and their families to thrive often failed. Sometimes, the methods he used—which were the methods he learned to use in his psychotherapeutic training—seemed to make matters worse. Already out-

of-control children were escalating bad behaviors. Parents (and teachers) felt more and more helpless. And during that time, more and more children were being put on Ritalin and other drugs when therapy didn't bring the situation under control.

Glasser began to work intuitively, discarding all that didn't work to help his young patients embrace their intensity and heal from their pasts as "bad kids." Over time, he developed a series of tools that worked with even the most difficult children. Not only did these children become better behaved; they seemed *transformed*. They were just as intense and alive as ever, but they had been led into a place where they wanted to use their intensity to succeed. Parents and teachers who learned and applied the approach found that it made them much more effective at drawing children out of patterns of rule-breaking and misbehavior and into patterns of ever-increasing success and happiness. They found that the NHA helped them cultivate more positive, mutually rewarding relationships with other adults as well.

At this writing, tens of thousands of households, hundreds of schools, and even a few school systems are applying the NHA. Thousands of mental health professionals apply it to their therapy practices and their work with challenged adult and pediatric populations.

Teachers are using the NHA to increase the productivity of their frontline workers—their students. Children exposed to the NHA in the classroom come to enjoy attending school; they participate more and increase their academic success because they truly want to learn. Suspensions drop, parent-teacher conversations about negative behaviors are reduced, and student trips to the office are reduced or eliminated. In schools where the NHA is applied, teacher retention has increased.

The NHA is a proactive approach to relationship that helps to circumvent time-consuming conflicts and disciplinary actions, whether it's applied in a workplace or in a school. When it's applied in the education sector, there is often a need to increase curriculum. **It enhances efficiency in the workplace too, allowing more to be accomplished in less time by reducing interpersonal conflicts and rule-breaking.**

The Nurtured Heart Approach in the workplace creates what Señora Corazon calls the Positivity Pulse. This pulse, sent through the vessel of the Nurtured Heart Approach, creates a feeling of connectedness—where workers feel engaged with the workplace, with their leaders and with each other.

In alignment with the concept of the heart-centered workplace, the NHA has a spiritual component too.

A Spiritual Relationship Revolution

Thanks to the rising popularity of hatha yoga in the West, the Sanskrit word *namaste* has hit the mainstream. Having spent some time immersed in South Asian culture in the early part of my psychology training, I heard this word many times before I actually understood its meaning. I really *got* it when I attended the Advanced Training in the Nurtured Heart Approach with Howard Glasser in Tucson, Arizona.

Graduates of this weeklong training become certified Nurtured Heart Specialists who can then take their learning out into their work as parents, educators, administrators, therapists, and consultants. Little did I know when I attended that it would be an intensely spiritual experience for most of the one hundred or so attendees from around the world. In the course of that week, I felt the true meaning of *namaste:*

I honor the place in you in which the entire Universe dwells.

I honor the place in you which is of Love, of Integrity, of Wisdom, and of Peace.

When you are in that place in you, and I am in that place in me, we are One.

Over the course of that week, we grew into a deeper understanding of and faith in the greatness within ourselves. As we recognized this about ourselves and others, we experienced the oneness in which we all dwell.

This is the foundation that supports the approach you will learn in this book: **an acceptance that greatness dwells within every person, including ourselves,** and that this greatness, when focused upon, will grow and deepen. **To focus on greatness, we develop a facility for talking about it in vivid and honest detail. As we learn to do this, we create relationships with others that are rooted in our mutual greatness.**

Greatness is what we all have in common, and celebrating it only creates more. It's boundless. And, as Glasser would say, whom does it hurt to point out the truth of the greatness in people around you? Whom does it hurt to recognize the greatness in yourself? Despite the answers most people give to these questions, a prevailing wind of negativity holds court in many small businesses, schools, nonprofit organizations, and corporate environments. Acknowledging, accepting, and consciously growing greatness in ourselves and others in the midst of all this negativity is nothing less than revolutionary.

Corporations Are Perfect Places for Growth and Transformation

The pulse in your organization may be leaking negative energy for a multitude of reasons. One primary reason for negativity is the top-down mentality that has guided much of corporate life for so long. This model has also trickled down to smaller organizations and businesses. This mentality prohibits the building of the kind of strong relationships that can keep corporations afloat even in today's economy.

Most corporations require some level of healing transformation. For most, this entails a movement away from oppressive, potentially devastating top-down thinking that does not clearly recognize the worth and contribution of each individual. Even as human beings have broken the spirits of others in the workplace, we've known that this is counterintuitive and counterproductive. **At any time, as gatekeepers of our work worlds, we can take responsibility for changing the way we relate to our staff, our students, our management teams, and our organizations**.

The tools in this book are tools for effective communication and relationship that will shift emphasis from problems and conflict to the greatness shared by CEOs and frontline workers alike. These tools will help you and your colleagues to step confidently out of a place of negativity and to create a much more positive environment. Instead of making demands, barking orders, and using tactics that instill fear, we can lead through positivity and with heart—but only if we have the guidance we need to change our ways.

Building Positive Institutions

As one of the first three hundred in the world to be trained by Dr. Marty Seligman from the University of Pennsylvania in his vanguard group, I have used positive psychology in the workplace for almost a decade in my leadership roles. Seligman set the stage for the impetus behind today's academic Positive Psychology movement where the the science of happiness is researched. The three pillars of the movement are: positive emotion, positive individual traits and positive institutions.

Positive psychology leader Barbara Fredrickson, PhD, describes how positive emotions build on themselves. Fredrickson makes a strong case that by increasing the opportunity to build positive emotion, we increase an employee's resources through enhancement of mindfulness, social support, self-acceptance, and increased sense of purpose.

In my own experience with positive psychology in the workplace, I've seen firsthand how increasing positive emotion enhances the ability to think lucidly and levelheadedly. This, in turn, leads to smart business decisions, increased team cohesiveness and productivity and improved workplace relationships. Research even demonstrates that positivity in the workplace yields decreased reports of illness! And research posits that it is more cost-effective to improve an existing employee's performance than to invest in the recruitment of a new staff member.

In her book, Fredrickson describes research from the University of California at Berkeley's Haas School of Business that "examined how positivity affects managers. They found that managers with greater positivity were more accurate and careful in making their decisions, and were more effective interpersonally. Other studies show that managers with greater positivity infect their work groups with greater positivity as well, which in turn produces better coordination among team members and reduces the effort needed to get their work done." (p.60)

Positive emotions aid in stress management practice by aiding people who were previously stressed relax back to their physiological baseline. **It makes sound business sense to focus on building positive emotion and to increase inner wealth.** This fosters a sense of flourishing that prevents languishing in the workplace.

In her book *Positivity: Groundbreaking Research Reveals How to Embrace the Hidden Strength of Positive Emotions, Overcome Negativity, and Thrive* (Crown Books, 2009), positive psychology leader and University of North Carolina-Chapel Hill psychology professor Barbara Fredrickson writes:

> Like any other living thing, you may languish, barely holding on to life, or flourish, becoming ripe with possibility and remarkably resilient to hard times…Striving to flourish…[is] not just about making yourself happy. It's about doing something valuable with your day and with your life…transcending self-interest enough to share and celebrate goodness in others. (p.17)

In workplaces where an environment of positivity is not present, languishing is a common experience for employees. A participant in one of my workshops shared the sad story of her own languishing, which strongly affected her level of effectiveness and her motivation to do her job well. It demonstrates how even subtle negativity can derail people in the workplace.

I was hired as a director for a multimillion-dollar agency. My specific role was to link the agency to various resources within the community for the benefit of the clients that we served. I had the expertise, knowledge, schooling, and personality to make me a huge success at what I was hired to do; I came highly recommended and I was hired on the spot during my initial interview. Eagerly, I accepted this new position, which was going to add substantially to the annual salary I'd earned with my previous employer (with whom I'd worked for twelve years). I anticipated that my skills and interests would be recognized and embraced in my new workplace.

My first year or two within the agency was great. I learned so much as I connected with stakeholders, and I gained the respect of the staff as I began to do presentations about the agency. Life was good; I was soaring.

On my second or third performance evaluation, the scores were good, but one comment troubled me. It was a short paragraph down from the part about how my superior constantly receives accolades via mail and telephone regarding my work for the agency. The comment read:"She shows great initiative but needs to communicate more effectively with her supervisor in terms of her tasks."

This confused me. I knew I had communicated with my supervisor about my tasks. But it seemed that those communications had fallen on deaf ears. Still, based on this bit of feedback, the CEO felt compelled to make a directive: I now had to e-mail him prior to every single appointment and wait for his approval before I showed up at that appointment. I was also told that I should "never meet with CEOs of agencies" because "CEOs should only meet with CEOs."

In the case of our agency, it would have been inappropriate for me to meet with line staff regarding operational or programmatic details. Besides, I would have thought that our CEO would be glad to have staff capable of interfacing with CEOs to exchange thoughts and ideas and to establish meaningful working relationships. And this particular CEO had little time to do this; in addition, he had been cited as "very rude" in the past. But my utmost respect for his authority kept me quiet. I simply did what I was told.

We moved forward, but I was frustrated. I began to notice our CEO's micromanaging style. He made a clear confession to me: that yes, he knew that I could make connections with important people, but that he had to show our Board of Directors that he could do the same! This helped explain the mysterious and inaccurate comment on my review.

Having grown up and lived my whole adult life in this same community, I had easily established relationships with the stakeholders with whom I no longer was allowed to relate in the way that made sense to me—the way in which I felt most skilled, and that had yielded such benefits to the company. My job had once been easy for me; but I was being told to sit down so my superior would have a chance to shine.

Under these circumstances, my spirit for the position died. This trickled down to every other aspect of work I was expected to perform for the agency. My enthusiasm dwindled, as did my initiative. I didn't even really want to get up and come to work on time, interface with staff or even look at our CEO. At the same time, I felt trapped, having brought myself and my family up to a new standard of living with my big salary jump.

What should I do with my feelings of misery in a position that once excited me? If I flat out told my CEO how I was feeling, would that be considered disrespectful? If I appeared to be bored, unhappy, or rebellious, would that be grounds for termination? Technically, I should have simply been fired because I had stopped doing the job I had been hired to do. Instead, for two more years, I sat quiet as a mouse, feeling disrespected by staff who thought I had a "cake" job where I did little to nothing. It wasn't that all of my responsibilities were taken from me; I had become rebellious, not wanting to do anything related to my position unless I was specifically told to do so. I felt like crap and contemplated leaving many times. But in an economy where layoffs are much more common than hires, where was I to go?

This experience has strongly affected me in other aspects of my life. I am not as social as I used to be. And even when I am, it's usually a façade of some kind where I'm just trying to get through the event. I am a bit more reserved as a person simply because what I loved to do was not embraced. It was not massaged or nourished. Who knows what I could be contributing to the world if my wings had not been clipped?

Seeking and building the greatness of my staff has always come naturally to me, as has a purposeful intention to create a positive institution. I try to find ways to handle setbacks and difficulties with genuine, heartfelt concern. When employees violate policies or procedures or under-perform, my ultimate aim is to get them back on track, where they can function as an integral part of the team. In the position I left to start my own company, I started out having been taught a different tack regarding disciplinary action, but believed indubitably that the way to reach full compliance and job satisfaction was to build strong relationships with and among my staff members.

Thanks to a progressive Chief Operations Officer who completely believed in my ability to lead in my own unique way, I was afforded the opportunity to participate in the Vanguard Positive Psychology Authentic Happiness Coaching Program under the leadership of Dr Martin Seligman and Ben Dean, Mentor Coach. I hungrily devoured the weekly lessons I learned and applied the exercises immediately with my staff. I literally went from the lecture into a staff meeting and began to plant positivity seeds. They in turn soaked up those lessons with open minds and hearts and we created a team that was unstoppable. To this day, almost ten years later, their connection is so strong that they still reach out to me and to one another, despite my having personally left that company in 2004. The essence of those relationships is just as vibrant today as it was then. Some of those staff have even followed me into my own company—an honor I hold to be one of the greatest I've ever received.

When starting out as a manager, I sought to build a leadership style that supported the foundation of a positive institution. I wished to find ways to broaden and build staff into their optimal realms of professional development without turning a blind eye to challenging workplace behavior—and I wanted to meet challenges from a place within my heart. From three decades of working in various institutions, I knew clearly that punitive styles of discipline were doomed to failure. I knew intuitively that top-down leadership was oppressive and counterproductive. Back then, my quest was a lonely one, and I did not have the precision tools of the Nurtured Heart Approach. It was all trial and error.

Since that time, the positive psychology movement has expanded, offering a wealth of tools to leaders who wish to forge a path away from top-down leadership and punitive discipline. The precision tools of the Nurtured Heart Approach provide a highly effective, easy-to-learn complement to positive psychology methods.

Chapter 3

Nurtured Heart Foundations

Remember, your most valuable resources drive away at the end of every business day, and it is your job to make sure they are eager to return the next morning.
–Kevin and Jackie Freiberg

The Nurtured Heart Approach is, at its root, about cultivating inner wealth in relationship. When we relate to others, we can use its tools to see greatness and to fluently talk about what we see. And we can use those same tools to see and talk about greatness in ourselves. The learning curve of the approach is about developing the ability to see and colorfully acknowledge success.

To make this happen, you'll learn:

- Four foundational concepts (in this chapter);

- Three stands (in chapter four), and

- Four techniques (in chapter five).

The concepts support the stands; together, they'll provide you with the theoretical underpinnings of the approach. Once you've grasped those concepts and stands, the techniques give you the tools to *live* those theoretical notions and to teach them to others.

Don't worry too much about grasping this right now. Let's plunge right into those foundational concepts, which might seem a little silly or random at first. Be patient: it all fits together as you move forward in learning the approach.

Four Foundational Concepts

I. *We are our employees' favorite toys.*

For children, parents or caregivers are their favorite toys. No other toy can match what they can do. They express countless emotions, expressions and energies in response to children's behaviors. Children watch carefully from infancy to see what their favorite toys do in response to their choices, both good and bad, and the figurative lights, sounds and vibrations of that toy teach them how to get the greatest possible validation and reinforcement from adults. This is how children learn to conduct themselves in the world.

As social beings, we continue to require love and attention—and not only from friends, partners, and family members. That desire follows us into the workplace, and because leaders have an authoritative role there, they become employees' "favorite toys."

A great deal of research in industrial and organizational psychology speaks to the validity of relationship in the workplace. This research demonstrates that the primary motivation to do good work and *As social beings, we do not stop wanting relationship when we become adults. The desire to be connected is inherent within us.*

cultivate good relationships is not financial. **Having a voice, feeling valued, and feeling connected are the real key factors that inspire team members to create happiness and greatness within an organization.** Employees are constantly looking to leadership for feedback and reinforcement in the form of energy and attention. In this way, we can think of ourselves as "toys" from which team members want to get as much energized relationship as possible.

Employees make choices based in large part on their desire to see leaders light up in response to those choices. For some, bad choices get made out of the sheer desire to get *some* kind of reaction from this favorite toy, because success doesn't seem to make the toy's bells and whistles go off in any reliable sort of way.

When team leaders find ways to see and verbally acknowledge success—or, as Glasser would say, *energize* success—team members come to recognize that their favorite toys will predictably light up and make fun sounds in response to their good choices.

KEYS TO SUCCESS

Find ways to give energy, response and relationship for the good stuff, just like Señora Corazon and the Nurtured Heart Warriors Team.

Perhaps you take the same view as Mrs. Crabtree did in the previous chapter: employees shouldn't get positive feedback just for doing what they're supposed to do in order to earn their paychecks. This brings us to the second foundational concept of the Nurtured Heart Approach.

2. *Shamu: Catching Success and Goodness vs. Creating Success and Greatness*

Have you had the pleasure of seeing an orca whale leap over a rope in a marine park performance? If you have, you might have wondered how human beings have been able to persuade a thirty-thousand-pound leviathan—the most famous of which was Shamu, a female orca whale who was trained to perform at the original Sea World in the 1960s—to do this kind of trick. Subsequent orca performers have been given the same name and they continue to perform at Sea World parks. As it turns out, the tricks used to train Shamu and her namesakes can be applied to human behavior in both private and public sectors.

If you think that Shamu's training involves being lured over the rope with a food reward, you're right. The key here is the placement of the rope. Do the trainers start with the rope high in the air? No—because the chances of coaxing her to leap for a fish right off the bat are slim. Do they put the rope along the surface of the water, perhaps? Just beneath the surface? No on both counts. The trainers wisely lay the rope as low as they possibly can: *along the very bottom of the pool.*

Once the rope is placed, the trainers wait for Shamu to cruise across it on her own. As soon as she does, she receives plenty of energized reward in the forms of food and affection. With consistent rewards given each time Shamu crosses the rope, this highly intelligent creature soon learns to elicit those rewards from her human friends by crossing the rope on purpose. Once that connection is made, the rope is incrementally raised...and eventually, although it's stretched high above the pool, Shamu continues to exert her will to leap over it so that she can receive those rewards.

This speaks to the importance of energizing, rewarding, and celebrating success every step of the way with your employees—highly intelligent creatures in their own right. It speaks to the importance of starting that figurative rope at the bottom of the pool: of finding ways to *create* success instead of "catching" it. If we set our expectations high and fail to reinforce employees if they don't soar and excel beyond those expectations, we miss infinite chances to nurture their greatness. And if we bring negative energy whenever they fail to soar to great heights of achievement—as Mrs. Crabtree did with Justice—a prevailing environment of negativity is created, socking employee and employer into a power struggle that serves no one and has destructive impact on both.

KEYS TO SUCCESS

Reinforce and energize team members for following rules; for showing good judgment; for living values like thoughtfulness, responsibility, respectfulness, conscientiousness, creativity, or generosity. Even small successes beget further success, and before you know it, employees are leaping to ever-greater heights of their own accord, just as Isabella was able to do under the guidance of the Nurtured Heart Warriors leadership team.

The Nurtured Heart Approach gives tools for seeing and acknowledging success, *no matter what*. Every time Shamu swims over that rope—no matter how low it lies beneath the water—success is created. The NHA teaches us to take every opportunity to create successes *that would otherwise not exist*. If we find ways to honor employees for what isn't wrong, we have a whole lot more to celebrate.

Celebrate what's *not* going wrong? Create success that would otherwise not exist? How does one do this without being a total Pollyanna, pink-washing the world and ignoring problems? Consider the tale of the Toll Taker, the next foundational principle of the Nurtured Heart Approach.

3.   Toll Taker: Choosing the Way We See Things

In his presentations and books, Howard Glasser shares a story about a dancing toll taker on the San Francisco Bay Bridge. The professor who originally told Glasser this story reported that he had driven over to the dancer's lane to pay his toll. "It looks like you're having the time of your life," the professor told the toll taker. The toll taker replied, "Of course! I have the best job in the world and the best office in the world." He colorfully describes the beautiful views he drinks in daily. He gets to see sunrises and sunsets while on the job—and, as luck would have it, he's an aspiring dancer who gets paid to practice in his glass-walled office high above the water! When the professor inquires about the other toll takers who don't seem so energized, the dancing toll taker responds, "Oh, those guys in the stand-up coffins? They're no fun!"

We get to choose how we see things. The toll taker could have focused on the difficult aspects of his job: long days on his feet, car exhaust, disgruntled commuters. That's what the guys in the stand-up coffins are likely focusing on. He chooses, instead, to dwell on what's right about where he is and what he's doing. The best part is that we get to make this choice in any moment of any day. No matter how much we've dwelled on the negative in the past, each new moment is an opportunity to see and acknowledge what's right in our worlds and in those around us.

Choosing to focus on what's right is about getting out of the way and allowing problems to solve themselves. By making this choice, we set intentions to climb to ever-greater heights of success instead of wallowing in negativity.

Making that choice is a leap of faith, because most of us are so conditioned to worry and doubt. But the reality is that worry and doubt don't solve problems.

Upon leaving home and helm to attend Howard Glasser's one-week advanced training in Tucson, I was plagued with worries and doubts. Due to technological challenges with a cell phone, I had to get a new one days before leaving for Arizona. My first opportunity to personalize it came while I sat in the airport prior to departure. The picture on the BlackBerry® screen wasn't appealing to me, and my curiosity took me to the other alternative. Lo and behold…it was a bridge, illuminated by the breathtaking colors of a coastal sunset! Every color of the rainbow glistened off the water beneath the glorious arches of that bridge. I knew right then and there I had to reset myself away from worries and doubts. I remembered the toll taker's story and saw that backdrop as a sign that following my dream to take this training was exactly what I supposed to be doing.

If I'd been in a different frame of mind, I would not have seen the profound symbolism of that bridge that appeared on my BlackBerry's screen. As it was, I was prepared to see it as a beautiful sign and as encouragement to follow my vision. It's all in how we see things.

As it turned out, the decision to attend this training and to enhance my knowledge and application of this approach was enormously meaningful. It gave me exactly the precision tools required to transform my entire organization into a positive institution.

4. *Game Theory: Clear Rules, Clear Consequences and Right Back in the Game of Greatness!*

Think back to the response of Justice's leaders when they caught him texting his girlfriend while on the job. One ignored the behavior, although he clearly saw it. Another called him on it, but relented when Justice assured him that it was just a quick message. And then, another member of Team Chrysalis gave him a full-on, sit-down-in-my-office lecture and threatened further disciplinary action. All three of these leaders saw the same infraction, but their reactions couldn't have been more different.

When leaders fail to strictly and clearly delineate and enforce rules, they enable and allow rule-breaking and the pushing of boundaries around rules. This is a surefire recipe for negativity as some employees dance around the rules to see how far they can push them. This isn't because employees are ill intentioned or bad people; it's just the natural pull of that uncertainty. They are seeking connection with leaders. It's up to leadership to refuse to connect with them around negativity and to instead choose, consistently and firmly, to create connection around greatness.

The Nurtured Heart Approach's answer is to hold up video games as a model for effective rule-making and enforcement. These games are set up to offer continuous positive reinforcement in the form of points, sounds, and visuals for as long as the player is successful. When a rule is broken or the player loses the game, the positive reinforcement stops…but all it takes to get back in the game is a simple reset, and the whole thing starts over.

For those of us who were born too early to have gotten on the video game bandwagon, pinball might be a better example. Imagine yourself standing at the pinball machine, wailing away at that little metal ball. Bells and whistles are going off and points are accumulating at astonishing rates. Then, you miss a beat and the ball falls into a hole. This round's over, and the bells, whistles, and points stop temporarily. But then…another ball pops up, and you're ready to get right back into the game of greatness by beginning again. No consequences, no punishment, no penalty—just an unceremonious reset to the next round.

Think about your favorite sport. How are the rules enforced? In response to a foul, an immediate penalty is imposed. In response to a broken rule or a lost point, sports referees generally blow a whistle, call it what it is, and get the players right back in the game.

Repeated infractions require more stringent action, but those actions are taken without a great deal of energy. The whole thrust is toward getting back to playing the game. So, with this in mind, how might Team Chrysalis react to Justice's infraction in a way that would present a unified front—and that would energize Justice to greatness instead of causing him to feel isolated, unmotivated and ashamed? In the Nurtured Heart Approach, the response to a broken rule is a simple, un-energized reset or time-out, just like those in video games, pinball, or sporting events—and a warmhearted welcome back to success as soon as rule-breaking stops. This technique will be described in much greater detail later on.

For now, suffice it to say that game theory in the NHA is about clearly enforcing rules without energizing rule-breaking, and about encouraging rule compliance by energizing that compliance while it is happening.

KEYS TO SUCCESS

We choose to clearly define rules and to consistently refuse to energize the breaking of rules (or the pushing of boundaries around rules). When consequences are necessary, we give them in an un-energized fashion. All energized response comes when rules are not being broken.

This, together with the intention to energize success, is the Nurtured Heart Approach's *default setting*. We energize success and refuse to energize negativity.

Believe In Yourself and Your Ability to Transform Your Workplace

> The key to your impact as a leader is your own sincerity. Before you can inspire with emotion, you must be swamped with it yourself.
> Before you can move their tears, your own must flow.
> To convince them, you must yourself believe.
>
> —*Winston Churchill*

If the idea of making a shift to positivity in your workplace appeals to you, first, you need to change *your* mind. Right now. You need to set your intention to start seeing what's right instead of what's wrong in your workplace.

Here's the good news: just by virtue of reading this far, you already *are* demonstrating that intention to change the way you see things. But this shift to positivity is deeper than any paradigm. To truly manifest that pulse of positivity in your organization, you'll need to work against the hardwiring of your brain.

Do you have a fear of snakes? What about spiders? Rodents? For people who fear these creatures, even a photograph of one—or the *thought* of one—can be enough to trigger a classic fight-or-flight response. Evolutionary psychology teaches that these kinds of fears are remnants of our hardwiring to notice any hint of danger. In *You Are Oprah,* Glasser shares with us a statement from Martin Seligman, the psychologist who set the impetus for today's modern-day study of positive psychology:

The part of the brain that triggers fear is primitive. It can't recognize that a photograph of a spider isn't dangerous or that a pet mouse or snake in a cage will not do harm. It also can't get that the worries, miseries, and doubts of everyday life are not actual threats to life and limb.

We don't want to change that part of the brain, because in times of true danger, it's absolutely necessary. Healthy negative emotions are essential for emotional and societal well-being. Without healthy anger and frustration, we would not be able to distinguish between right and wrong. Without these emotions, we would be hard-pressed to find the energy to fight for justice and speak out about wrongdoing. However, in order to allow the positivity pulse to move through us, we need to make a habit of accessing higher-functioning parts of the brain—the frontal lobes, which handle (among other things) *executive function.* Executive function enables humans to selectively pay attention, plan behaviors, choose how they'll respond to whatever happens to them, and apply their intelligence to solving problems.

> *Because our brain evolved during a time of ice, flood, and famine, we have a catastrophic brain. The way the brain works is looking for what's wrong. The problem is, that worked in the Pleistocene era...but it doesn't work in the modern world. (p. 32)*

Step into your frontal lobes. Give more power to this part of your brain in order to be the change you want to be. The NHA demands that you zero in on *what is going right*. It's up to you, as a leader, to take the initiative in learning how to do this—to confidently choose positivity for your workplace. Doing so will empower you within your mind and heart to apply the stands and recognitions you'll learn about in the next sections of this book.

KEYS TO SUCCESS

The new fight and flight: Fight to change your way of thinking. Fight for shifting your mind toward positivity and step back and savor that flight to success as you transform your workplace. Be grateful for the changes in you that are the changes you wish to see.

Chapter 4

Identifying the Three Stands: Clear-Cut Commandments

The stands are the support system of this approach. Any time you aren't sure how to react or act, checking back in with your three stands will give you direction and resolve. The techniques described in subsequent sections all work to uphold these stands.

In taking the first stand, we resolve to **energize success no matter what.** In taking the second stand, we resolve to **enforce rules strictly but nonpunitively.** And in taking the third stand, we resolve that we'll **refuse to give energy to negativity**—choosing instead to reset ourselves and others to the greatness that's inherent in all. When these three stands are adhered to with unwavering conviction, the energy in your workplace will quickly shift.

> **Stand One:**
>
> **Resolve to purposefully create and nurture success and greatness.**
> **Relentlessly, strategically draw your team members into new and renewed patterns of success and greatness.**

Think back to the stories of Shamu and the toll taker. We get to set the rope as low as we like in order to catch and create successful moments. We get to choose how we see things—whether we see what's right or what's wrong. Once that resolution is made, we use the techniques for creating and energizing success that are given on pages 47-49.

> ## Stand Two:
> **Resolve to have clear rules and clean, consistent, effective consequences when those rules are broken.**

The Nurtured Heart Approach is not a "soft" approach. It doesn't entail singing employees' praises when they're breaking rules. It's about knowing the rules cold; about reinforcing and encouraging team members for *not* breaking them; and about being absolutely consistent about giving a consequence whenever rules are broken. It's also about moving right on to the next moment of success, just as we do when playing pinball or when we're done with the penalty invoked during a sporting event. We don't give energy to the problem of a broken rule—on the contrary, problems get no emotional play, no backlash, no long-term repercussions. Just a reset and then an openhearted invitation back to the greatness that was always there.

Whether you are enforcing rules or giving out positive recognitions, you are playing hardball with this approach. You're relentlessly nurturing hearts and playing this game to *win!* Take these stands with determination. Let your competitive edge—which you must have if you've come this far in the corporate world or within your organization as a leader—drive you to be RELENTLESS and FEARLESS about applying this approach. Just as we refuse to forget to energize success (Stand One), we refuse to look the other way when someone is breaking a rule (Stand Two).

Begin to manifest this Stand by stating rules in *negative language*. This makes "in-bounds" and "out-of-bounds" absolutely clear. For example:

Blow the dust off that policy and procedure manual and get to know your company's rules. When a rule is broken, acknowledge this without bells, whistles, lectures, or

NO personal cell phone use

NO coming in late

NO escalating conflicts

NO negative attitude

NO talking in meetings

NO sarcastic comments

NO racist, sexist, homophobic, ageist, or religious jokes or comments.

NO unprofessional attire

warnings. If you've stepped on the line, you've broken the rule; if you haven't, you can be praised for that choice. *Period!* And don't worry about holding a meeting to go over new rules or a new way of stating old rules. Teach rules by (first) recognizing employees for *not* breaking them, and by (when necessary) enforcing them when they're broken.

How do we enforce? By *withdrawing energetic connection*. Enforce a broken rule with as little energy, emotion, and drama as possible. When Mrs. Crabtree engaged Justice with a long lecture, she demonstrated to him that her energy was most accessible in response to the breaking of a rule. It might not have been pleasant for Justice, but it gave him something he felt he needed: an intense connection with someone on the leadership team. He hadn't found a way to that connection by following rules.

To avoid this dynamic, refuse to give your precious energy to problems—just reset the rule breaker and find a way to welcome him into the next success.

By choosing to energize what's right, we show team members that their favorite toys do lots of cool stuff when they are successful, and that those toys get boring when they break rules, push boundaries, or fail to show up as the great beings they are.

Stand Three:

Refuse to leak negativity.

Not sure what a negativity leak might look like? It's happening any time you demonstrate that:

- ✓ problems, issues, and broken rules captivate and elicit your charged interest;

- ✓ you expect an employee to do something wrong;

- ✓ you are willing to focus energy and attention on poor choices;

- ✓ by making poor choices or breaking rules, employees are able to access the "buttons" that deliver energized relationship;

- ✓ that relationship and "love" in the form of recognition flow more strongly as a result of the employee doing something less than acceptable—leading the employee to perceive, at a deep, subconscious level, that more recognition is available in response to wrong behavior.

The NHA posits that leaking negativity undermines the efficacy of the approach. This being said, know that *everybody leaks*. This approach does not require perfect execution; we're all human, and we all make mistakes and leak negative energy. *It's how we rebound from that mistake or leakage that makes the difference*. As soon as you notice a leak, you can change course and step cleanly into a new moment of positivity. The techniques described in the next chapter will show you how.

Chapter 5

Learn the Methods: The Strategies that Support the Stands

Use the following tools to consistently recognize and notice positivity. Because they involve capturing a moment of success in real time, just as you'd do when snapping a photograph, three of the four are named after cameras.

Strategy 1: Active Recognitions (Kodak Moments)

Clearly observe what the employee is doing when he or she is acting positively. Offer a "verbal snapshot" of what you see. Avoid any kind of judgment:

"I notice you're at work early today."

"I see that our client got you really frustrated, and you stayed calm and professional."

"I notice how you are all working together on that project."

Even if the employee is sitting there doing nothing, or if he's just doing what he's supposed to be doing, consider all the ways in which he's being successful and making choices that are positive. Although most of us aren't accustomed to acknowledging others for the little things they do right, this technique is a great way to start creatively doing so—to activate those new neural pathways to positivity.

In the NHA, these are also referred to as "video moments" because in these moments, we are simply reflecting back to the employee what the lens registers. We're relaying the picture exactly as we see it and calling out the positive attributes being demonstrated. The person feels irrefutably noticed, acknowledged, and appreciated for doing what she is supposed to be doing—working, following rules, and showing positivity.

In giving these simple recognitions we are beginning to "hardwire" the brain in a new way. We're establishing neural circuits that will allow us to take the approach deeper with added texture and compassion as we move into the next three techniques, all of which build on the first one.

At another level, the person feels that her very existence is being acknowledged as an important part of the workplace—recognized and held in esteem just for showing up.

Remember Mr. Kodak of the Nurtured Heart Warriors Team? He actively recognizes and notices even small details. He's exceedingly generous with these "Kodak moments," taking "snapshots" like an instant camera practically everywhere he goes:

- ♥ "Jan, I see how hard you are working."

- ♥ "José, I notice you got very angry with that customer before, and you kept calm."

- ♥ "Shana, it was wonderful that you shared those great ideas with us today."

- ♥ "Jim, I notice how caring you are about your co-workers."

- ♥ "Michael, you are doing great at multitasking today. Thanks for asking for that checklist to help you stay organized."

- ♥ "Brenda, you are so wonderful at reorganizing yourself after a big project gets us off course."

   As soon as a new employee starts work, Active Recognition can be used to begin to cultivate and nurture the relationship between him and other staff members. Starting a new position can bring anxiety; confidence can be low in the early days of this new journey. The use of Active Recognition promotes engagement and healthy organizational socialization for a new employee.

- ♥ "Dimitrius, welcome aboard. I notice you seem to be looking for something. How may I help?"

- ♥ "Carly, I can see you have really taken your time to learn our policies and procedures with all your notes."

- ♥ "ToniAnne, it's clear to me you are so excited to learn new things."

When given in place of the usual rushed salutation, an Active Recognition can be quite meaningful in a person's life. Active Recognition powerfully states that you value that employee for who he or she is in that moment. Many times employees have described feelings of invisibility in the workplace; Active Recognition turns this energy upside down, proving that no one in the workplace is invisible—that they are seen and even celebrated each time they walk through the door.

Workplaces of every size and type have not only a legal, ethical responsibility but a moral responsibility to build and respect diversity in the workplace. With an Active Recognition, you can easily segue into a brief conversation with someone about differences and similarities in ethnicity, cultural norms, language, clothing, or traditions.

Active Recognitions are also invaluable for igniting conversations that can lead to cultural awareness and competency. When done without judgment, simply as a respectful recognition of difference, this shows respect and interest and can open up heartfelt dialogue. This, in turn, cultivates understanding and good relationship, which then leads to increased productivity. Research has shown that diverse teams are more productive. Active Recognitions set the stage for enhancing recognition, conversation and positive regard around this element in your workplace.

- ♥ (To an employee who brings a traditional Indian dish from home) "Naveen, I see you've brought food from home for lunch today. It has such a rich aroma and it looks incredibly healthy. "

- ♥ (To a Muslim female employee who wears a traditional head covering to work) "Sarwat, that's such a colorful head scarf. It really brightens up the room!"

    Although Active Recognition is a rather easy, practical application, keep in mind that it is a new language requiring several unconventional communication dynamics on the part of both you and your team.

- ♥ "Nancy, I notice you are here early with a list for our meeting."

- ♥ "Connie, you are dressed very professionally today for our interviews."

- ♥ "Eric, you are working very quickly on that project and getting things in order."

Positivity Pulse Points: Active Recognition/Kodak Moments

Use Active Recognition/create Kodak Moments:

✓ Only for positive moments (remembering the toll taker: that if you choose, you can see positivity almost anywhere)

✓ Never in reference to rule-breaking or negative behavior

✓ By employing neutral, nonjudgmental language to make the message as "digestible" as possible

✓ With as much specificity and detail as possible

Strategy 2: Experiential Recognitions (Polaroids)

With this technique, we build on Active Recognitions by adding a description of the *values* being reflected in the employee's positive choices. With this strategy, capture the employee in the moment of *living* desirable values and demonstrating strengths. Through this, we build and reinforce character strengths and virtues.

Glasser and Block describe values as being attributes of the heart. They are behaviors or thoughts judged by society as what is intrinsically good or what is worthy of imitating. A list of values and strengths worth acknowledging might include:

Caring	Integrity
Compassion	Inventive
Commitment	Kindness
Confidence	Leadership
Consideration	Openheartedness
Cooperation	Open-mindedness
Courage	Patience
Creativity	Peace
Cultural sensitivity	Resolve
Determination	Resourceful
Expressiveness	Respect
Fairness	Responsibility
Good sportsmanship	Self-control
Hardworking	Team player
Helpfulness	Thoughtfulness
Honesty	Tolerance
Humility	Using good manners
Inner strength	Wisdom

When you use this type of recognition, you are amplifying Active Recognition by including a positive judgment and/or value attached to the statement. What values and strengths do you wish to acknowledge and strengthen in your workplace? Give recognitions and appreciations that are specific, detailed, and based on observable behavior.

In their book *Character Strengths and Virtues* (Oxford University Press, 2004), Christopher Peterson and positive psychology pioneer Martin Seligman expand on the notions of character, values, and virtues by creating categories of human strength:

- strengths of wisdom and knowledge
- strengths of courage
- strengths of humanity
- strengths of justice
- strengths of temperance
- strengths of transcendence

Consider how the values that are important to you might fall into these categories. On any given day, you can consciously choose which category you would like most to acknowledge in your workplace.

Or, try this exercise: have all of your employees identify their character strengths and virtues on www.authentichappiness.org, the Web site of Dr. Martin Seligman and his team at the University of Pennsylvania. As the leader, analyze this data to identify the major strengths of the team, derived from their top five signature strengths.

Remember Mrs. Polaroid, who flows gracefully in her ability to experientially recognize the people with whom she comes into contact daily. As a more seasoned manager, she has the ability to use positive judgments and value statements to develop and deepen characteristic strengths and virtues—and she does it in her own unique, intense style.

Experiential Recognition is a right-in-the-moment opportunity to anchor employees in the values, philosophy, policies, and procedures of the workplace. This is the piece that moves beyond the "thank you" or "great job" we have been using conventionally. Here we have the golden opportunity to further enforce a company's philosophy, vision, and mission statement as well as rules and regulations.

- ♥ "Jan, I see how hard you are working. You show such a strong work ethic!"

♥ "Tom, I noticed you got angry with that customer before, but you handled it with true professionalism and kept your cool."

♥ "Shana, it was wonderful that you shared those great ideas with us today at the meeting! This shows your leadership qualities. True teamwork."

♥ "Jim, I notice how caring you are about your co-workers. This shows your compassion and commitment to a positive workplace."

♥ "Michael, you are doing a great job at multitasking today. Thanks for asking for a checklist. This shows your willingness to want to do your job even better, and it's a great way to stay organized."

♥ "Brenda, you are so wonderful at reorganizing after a big project. This shows your amazing ability to get us back on track and shows you care so much about what you do here."

Positivity Pulse Points: Experiential Recognitions/Polaroids

To create a moment of experiential recognition:

✓ Start with an Active Recognition/Kodak Moment

✓ Add a comment that reflects a value or strength

✓ Apply this technique when a team member is doing a great job and/or following the rules

✓ Be genuine; show excitement (in your own way)

✓ Remember Shamu and the toll taker

Strategy 3: Proactive Recognitions/Canons

Proactive Recognition builds on both Active and Experiential Recognitions. To proactively recognize an employee, we notice and verbally acknowledge moments where he or she is *not breaking rules*.

This might sound absurd at first, but ultimately, this technique can be incredibly energizing! Intentional celebration of moments where problems are *not* occurring gives you a vast realm for positive reflections. Rather than giving energy to the person only when a rule is being broken or there's a threat of it being broken, this technique gives that energy in response to rules *not* broken. The employee comes to see that much positive attention is available in return for *remaining in compliance* with the organization's policies and procedures.

Proactive Recognition begins with our leaders in the workplace—that's you. Start with a complete grasp of the workplace's rules and policies, then state them precisely and negatively (starting with the word "No…"). Rules or policies may require modification to fit these parameters—if this is the case, then get to it!

Once those rules and policies have been established or re-established, they need to be clear and strictly upheld. Here are several examples of workplace rules:

- No personal cell phone use while working
- No coming late to work or back from breaks
- No personal use of Internet while working
- No changing deadlines for projects
- No smoking in front of the building
- No gossiping about one another
- No cross talking in meetings
- No passive-aggressive statements
- No teasing

Proactive recognition inspires employees to comply with rules, regulations and policies without adversarial relationship. It accelerates and deepens the refusal to energize negativity, moving the employee into a new realm of success and counteracting the tendency to create energized relationship around noncompliance. Recognitions will differ as workplace philosophies, policies, and procedures differ, allowing for great flexibility in tailoring the technique to individual workplaces. It's a great way to tap into heart-centered proactivity and to gently reset away from negative reactivity. And it creates vast realms of possible success that may have previously gone unrecognized.

A Positive Pulse with Policies and Procedures

Most employees want to remain in compliance; in general, they don't wish to upset their bosses. Still, as we all know, there are times when even the best intentioned person will push the limits. We all know that some of us are more inclined to do this than others, and that some of us have intrinsic natures that inspire us to push limits to a greater degree. Another way of putting this is that some of us will leak more negativity than others.

Recall Mrs. Crabtree's all-too-typical attitude about acknowledging the positive choices of staff: "Why do we need to thank someone for what they're supposed to be doing? That's what they get paid for." I didn't pull this quote out of thin air; a boss of mine once said this to me. He was the vice president of our department and I was next in line, deemed the division director. When I was brought into that organization, I felt a strong pulse of negativity that made my heart skip beats and my stomach turn. Even the air was stifling. I was also dealing with a union house, which meant it was close to impossible to rid ourselves of staff who had no desire to change and who consistently violated policy under everyone's nose. I became determined to create positive change there.

In this environment, hours and hours were spent trying to change negative behavior. There were multiple meetings with union representatives and several managers. Some of those people were amazing human beings doing phenomenal work, but they didn't get any acknowledgement for this.

Our brains are wired this way. We've learned to respond to negativity vociferously while letting the positive slip under our radar. This habit bleeds into the ways in which we deal with children, and this is why many end up seeking out "negative attention"—because there is a bigger payoff for that than in moments when they're behaving well. The Nurtured Heart Approach works well for these children because it repeatedly demonstrates to them that they will be recognized for the positives and not so much for the negative, rule-breaking behaviors.

At no time in the course of these events did I hear a single statement of recognition or appreciation.

The Difficult Employee and the Underachieving Employee, Explained

Although adults would seem to be too evolved to act out to get attention in the way a child would, this isn't always the case. In the workplace, adult team members may fall into this same pattern. Some adults even seem to thrive on this negative attention and all the drama that surrounds it.

Often, co-workers and managers are baffled and challenged when dealing with this type of employee. Such an employee is generally aware that noncompliance may result in the loss of his or her job, but the need for energetic nourishment trumps this concern. If it's the only way to be energetically fed, he or she will go that route—although the quality of that nutrition is subpar and leaves the employee with a continuing feeling of lack and longing. When this kind of employee is placed into a chaotic, unstructured environment where rules are blurry and management is inconsistent, negative energy leak is exacerbated tenfold.

This employee becomes the energy leak in the system of the workplace.

Then there are the extremely compliant employees who come to work every day on time, return from breaks punctually, complete all their tasks, and generally do not get involved in workplace banter and gossip. While they are good employees, they are not *great* employees—because their workplace relationships do not inspire them. Because they're such "good" employees, they get almost no attention in the workplace. They don't make waves. These accommodating employees may think their ideas do not matter, because they have not been encouraged to come forth with those ideas.

They are a source of hugely untapped potential.

How many of us take receptionists or security staff for granted? These people are the gatekeepers for our workplace. Do we appreciate how challenging their workdays can be? Do we acknowledge them when they go above and beyond to hunt someone down in the face of an emergency or when they politely handle an irate customer? Is there any recognition that as the very first people seen by the rest of our employees and leaders in the morning, these frontline workers are the gateway to positivity—and that in this role, they have the power to set the tone and mood for each day? They are also the very first people with whom our customers come in contact when they walk through the door or call the company.

Imagine a workplace where every individual, at every level, is shining in goldenness and positivity, flourishing with creative ideas and brilliance that steadily increase their productivity. The workplace comes to shine because each individual is shining.

The point is that no matter what the position, everyone in the workplace has a right to be acknowledged and treated with dignity, respect, and integrity. In this very moment, they are participating in making that workplace run like a finely tuned engine. Everyone deserves proper nourishment and feedback for contributions to the Positivity Pulse in your organization. Every employee deserves to be energetically nourished for his or her role in the workplace.

Refuse to be sucked into creating energized relationship around problems, doubts, and worries; instead, set the intention to create a positive workplace where people want to participate and have positive, productive relationships.

When employees have challenges, shift the energy and find a way to create success in that moment. Envision that all employees who walk through the door of your organization to begin their workday feel acknowledged for their greatness. They feel great about being at work. Their leaders have learned how to create and celebrate successes both large and small.

As leaders, we become role models. It is incumbent upon us to set the tone—to create the pulse in our workplaces. This is never truer than in moments when we are being challenged by employees who are used to getting energized for poor choices.

This is where we are asked to step up and play the field fearlessly to catch that negative energy...and to swing as if we are going for the grand slam of our careers—to knock that negativity right out of the ballpark!

And no matter how firm we are on the first two Stands, it is natural for us to shift back to negative thinking and behavior from time to time, and to let that negativity "leak" out into our relationships.

Take a moment to think about the rule breakers in your workplace. Consider how differently they are treated by each leader—much as Justice got radically different responses from each member of Team Chrysalis. Some leaders would rather avoid conflict and take a "see no evil, hear no evil, speak no evil" approach. Others confront conflict head-on: dragging the employee into their offices, giving a lengthy lecture, spending time on a written warning, and otherwise investing significant time and emotional energy on reprimands and "if you *ever* do this again..." scenarios. Some will bring in a second manager, which cuts into productivity time—all to give energy to a rule breaker!

There are also those of us who attempt to sit down with a rule-breaking employee for a peaceful heart-to-heart about *why* rules were broken. I know all about this, because I've fallen into this trap myself. This approach might feel compassionate and loving, but I'd like to suggest that it's more loving to avoid dwelling on the problem.

We all have personal challenges, and those challenges often spill over into the workplace. This can cause rule-breaking. You might think you're showing that you care when you conduct what amounts to a private therapy session in your office, and the employee might have truly difficult issues on his or her plate, but what ends up happening is an intense energetic exchange around the breaking of a rule.

Although I want you to lead with your heart, I do not recommend letting your heart bleed when it comes to strict policy and procedure enforcement!

If you're a bleeding-heart sort, try this next time: reset yourself and refer the distressed employee to an employee assistance counselor through Human Resources. Your role is to immediately and unceremoniously address the rule broken with a reset, then assist that employee back to greatness—relentlessly and fearlessly.

As leaders, we need to explore the ways in which we have enabled negative behavior in our workplaces. Have we cast a blind eye on the problem? Have we remained silent instead of addressing rule-breaking in the moment—only to finally explode with negative energy in response to that rule being broken repeatedly? Only by getting honest about our role in creating workplace negativity can we change our behavior. Only by changing that can we change our entire workforce.

Some difficult employees may fail to respond positively to this approach. Give it your best try—that is, hold tight to the stands in the face of continuing or escalating negativity—to determine whether they are ready to transcend this resistance. Some may be in a place in their own world that makes this transition impossible for them, and if this is the case, an EAP referral may be called for.

With Proactive Recognition, as we focus on noticing when employees are *not* infracting policies, employees come to see policies and procedures not as restrictions or limitations, but as sources of positive attention and reinforcement—because the more they stay in compliance, the more recognition they receive.

Unceremoniously Addressing Negativity and Noncompliance: Reset Back to Greatness

What if a rule is not being followed? Time to give a simple, un-energized reset. Here's how the reset works. Let's say someone approaches you in the workplace and begins to gossip about another staff member. Simply state, "I'm going to reset you now," or just "Reset."

No lectures, no reminders, no warnings, no explanations. If he was gossiping, that employee knows full well why he was reset. And if there's any confusion about why the reset happened, you can clear it up as soon as the gossiping stops by giving a Proactive Recognition about the no-gossiping rule being followed.

Using the word *reset* gives us an opportunity to remind ourselves and our staff that we can reset ourselves away from negativity as soon as we realize it's happening. Think of it as a keyword that supports us in ridding ourselves of a negative cognition, negative behavior or an unhealthy negative emotion that arises as a knee-jerk reaction to that negativity.

This being said, "reset" isn't the only word used in this way by those who practice the Nurtured Heart Approach. You can select a different word that works for your organization. Choose one that holds this idea of pausing during a moment *When we reset others, we are not scolding them or trying to shame or embarrass them. We are reminding them that they have the power within themselves to get right back on track.* of rule-breaking and creating an opportunity to jump into a new moment of greatness. Find your own way to utilize this technique creatively. Some simply raise one hand silently and firmly to send the message that they are not energizing negativity—not even enough to speak about it or to listen. Even if it means running around the workplace blowing referee whistles or holding aloft a "Reset" paddle, find your own way to make the reset make sense in your workplace.

Some folks are having fun with the word *recalculate*, which reminds us of our inner GPS— that part of ourselves that calmly recalculates when we make a wrong turn and guides us back in the right direction.

During a confrontation, one of my staffers once said, "Well, if we're going to get into the finger-pointing game, then I guess I'll take the *In my work with a few Wall Street information technology leaders—one of whom is an MIT graduate—some have come to favor the word "reboot," which helps them to visualize a download of new, positive internal "software" to replace outdated negativity that no longer serves them.* blame." His tone was sarcastic, with undercurrents of anger and defensiveness. I responded, "Michael, reset. We need to focus on identifying a solution to ensure that we don't make the same mistake again." Instead of ignoring the sarcasm, I reset him. Instead of lecturing about having a positive attitude and how this is our philosophy in the workplace, I reset him. He knew why I did and he responded beautifully. After thanking him for his willingness to reset to finding constructive solutions to our workplace issue, we shifted our focus to identify the weak link in our system and to correct it.

A little later on in the day, Michael sent a text message apologizing for his negative behavior. At that point I reminded him there was no need because it was over—and that right then and there, in that moment, he was standing in his greatness, being peaceful, and contributing to a harmonious and productive workplace.

How great it feels, in a moment when negativity threatens to consume precious time and resources, to simply and efficiently reset onto a more positive path. Although the process can be playful and creative—even fun!—the reset is not meant to be humorous. It's about a serious intention to avoid getting mired down in negativity.

Expecting employees to be in compliance with policies and procedures regarding particular behaviors that cut into productivity—for example, gossiping and personal cell phone and Internet use—increases productivity and helps achieve workplace goals. This expectation is better served by an approach that celebrates multiple aspects of compliance rather than targeting lack of compliance.

Gossip is a major energy leak in many workplaces, and the reset is especially effective for dealing with it. When someone is gossiping or making negative statements about others, simply reset them. If you catch yourself giving those statements your attention and allowing them to infect the workplace, then you too require your own internal reset. Listening is participating. Listening perpetuates the negativity.

This particular recognition is extremely useful for keeping employees in compliance with policies and procedures—especially if they have had challenges with this. Don't forget Ms. Canon, the ultimate policy implementer and relentless rule follower at Creative Recognition, Inc. Through Proactive Recognition, she keeps her team in full compliance. When they're on task, she swiftly reminds them of how wonderful they are for NOT breaking the rules and for following policy! She appreciates team members' willingness to change old habits, to stay in healthy control, and to reset themselves to remain in compliance.

It is a proactive stance that keeps leaders in the moment and gives them a way to give heartfelt, grateful recognition when employees stay on task.

An interesting aside: the brand name of Canon was created in Japan in 1934. The word comes from Kwanon, the name of the Buddhist goddess of mercy (also known as Kwan Yin). In Buddhist scripture, Kwanon was a bodhisattva—one who is motivated by great compassion for the benefit of all human beings. One of the many translations of the Sanskrit word satva is "heroic-minded one"; bodhi means "enlightenment," "awakening," or "to know." Think about this recognition and the Nurtured Heart Approach overall as a means to enlighten your workplace and to take it to a higher level of consciousness. As you take this journey, feel yourself filled with compassion and great wisdom. Lead your company into optimal greatness for the benefit of all human beings. Be the servant leader.

Practice Resetting Yourself

One of the most powerful uses of the reset is in resetting our own thoughts away from negativity. Practice resetting yourself before you expel negative thoughts into spoken words or writing. Delete that sarcastic e-mail. Choose not to make that gossipy or confrontational comment. Let your co-workers know that you're just as prepared to reset yourself as you are to reset them. Say it out loud—"Oops! Time to reset myself!"—wipe the slate clean, and take yourself and your staff right back to the beat of the Positivity Pulse.

Personally, I have a tendency to embellish on topics and get off track. I have become quite aware of my intensity. I want to share all the knowledge in my head and give every last detail of my experience, but I realize that this is not necessary in some forums, and that I owe it to my audience to present this kind of material only when I've taken the time to organize it. If I find myself wandering or becoming overly intense during a meeting, I'll say, "I'm going to reset myself and get back on track in order for us to complete our agenda."

I'll do the same when a staff member gets off track and tries to keep pulling away from the topic or agenda by saying, "Maria, I need to reset you." At this point, I use other NHA techniques to acknowledge what's going right in the moment, and then we move on.

Because this is something I am working on transforming within me, I may make a statement to my team that I am sure they are happy that I am staying on task. "I took my own reset quite well," I'll say, "and I sure am glad I was able to do that. And, Maria, you gracefully accepted your reset and got right back into the game with us. Thanks for showing your commitment to helping to keep the momentum of our meeting going." This shows my willingness as a leader to admit that I too make mistakes—and that I can model the Positivity Pulse. It also shows clearly that I am not a top-down leader. I'm willing to realize publicly that I make mistakes, just like anyone else.

Let's take a look at Proactive Recognition in Action!

- ♥ "Brenda, thank you so much for getting to work on time. You set a good example in following this rule."

- ♥ "Michael, I know you got frustrated with that co-worker who did not do her job, but you remained calm. You didn't curse, and you were helpful. By staying in control, you're helping us maintain a positive and peaceful environment."

- ♥ "Sue, I heard your personal cell phone ringing, and noticed you didn't pick it up...then, you quickly put it in silent mode. Thank you for following our policy about personal cell phone use in the workplace!"

- ♥ "I notice you are staying well within the time frame for project completion. That's crucial! You're being successful in not falling behind."

- ♥ "I can see that are showing up several minutes before your shift starts. We appreciate your efforts to start work on time!"

- ♥ "I see you don't have your cell phone out and are not texting on work time. Thanks for following that rule. I know it's tempting...and you're not doing it!"

- ♥ "Thanks to all of you for not cross talking during the meeting. It really helps me stay focused and on point."

Reflect on the toll taker and Shamu. Choose to see rules followed and drop the rope as low as necessary to create success. Move away from reacting to rule-breaking and into proactive recognition of rules and procedures followed.

Negative reactivity comes from a primal place in our brains—from our stored emotional memory. Being proactive requires us to step up into our frontal lobes and to tap into our executive functions. As we do this, we move into our hearts easily and naturally. By choosing proactive positivity over reactive negativity, you are creating a peaceful environment that's not afflicted by the mental state of *kilesas*—an early Buddhist term that describes the temporary clouding of the mind, which then manifests in unskillful actions.

Lead by example. Make change by being, living, and breathing the change you want to be. Recognize any and all steps toward compliance with rules whether they are diminutive or statuesque—even if they are few and far between.

By employing the Nurtured Heart Approach, you are proactively responding from a place within your heart to bring peace and happiness to your workplace. You are well on your way to transforming your workplace to a place where people truly want to be.

Positivity Pulse Points: Proactive Recognitions/Canons

To give Proactive Recognitions:

✓ Define workplace policies and procedures as negative rules that start with the word "no"

✓ Be on the lookout for rules followed and make a point of recognizing employees for following the rules

✓ Talk about policies and procedures in the context of their being followed rather than only bringing them up when someone isn't following them

✓ Respond to rules broken or policies or procedures not followed with a reset—whether it's for someone else or for yourself

✓ Move right back into greatness by recognizing the next success

---

In today's trying times, employees need their workplace to be a safe haven where structure and a sense of peacefulness prevail, and this is the workplace you are striving to create. You are feeding your staff with the nectar of strong, healthy working relationships. You're doing so through positive recognition and appreciation of character strengths and virtues, and you are applying this approach with *intensity, relentlessness, fearlessness,* and *clarity*.

Strategy 4: Creative Recognition: Creating Successes That Would Not Otherwise Exist

Creative Recognition builds on Active Recognition, using clear, simple commands and bigger-than-ordinary positive acknowledgments in response to even small gradations of compliance. This inexorably draws the employee in a successful direction. Glasser writes that "it is the small and doable steps that pave the way to building success and training for bigger accomplishments."

Creative Recognition is a way of making those steps available and rewarding for even the most challenging employee. This technique makes success unavoidable—and leads the employee to trust that he'll get plentiful energized connection even in response to the smallest success.

For example:

♥ Anna gets to the office and heads for her desk. You might say, "Anna, I need you to go right to your workstation and get started; it's going to be a busy day." As soon as she sits down, give abundant recognition. "I see you're jumping right in. I so appreciate your energy and commitment."

♥ At a meeting, Jordan looks anxious and annoyed, as though he has something important he needs to say and is waiting for the right moment to chime in. "Jordan, I see you're itching to contribute, and I need you to wait until I get through this slide." He does. Then, ask for his input while giving recognitions: "I could see how frustrating it was for you to wait to volunteer your take on this issue. You demonstrated great patience, even when I asked you to wait a little longer. Thanks for contributing so much to the respectful atmosphere of this meeting."

In a broader sense, you might think of Creative Recognition as turbocharged creativity around finding ways to call employees out for being successful. Our employees' challenges with maintaining compliance come up for a multitude of reasons. By creatively recognizing our employees for *every increment* of compliance—in Shamu terms, getting that rope all the way to the bottom and then recognizing and acknowledging every movement in the direction of that rope—we are truly energizing them to want to be compliant with poli-

We as leaders contribute to that non-compliance when we avoid addressing the issue or confront rule violation in a way that merely energizes negativity.

cies and procedures and to uphold the quality standards we want in our workplace. We can also creatively recognize them for putting forth genuine effort, making difficult changes, overcoming obstacles, and staying on a trajectory of personal growth and ever-increasing achievement.

Glasser's concept of *notching it up* applies here: you're taking the approach to its hilt. You're putting rope all over Shamu's tank, making success impossible to avoid. You're opening the mind of the toll taker yet further to the glory of a job that might seem menial to someone less attuned to the positive side of things.

♥ "Jim, I know this change was challenging for you. I truly appreciate your change of heart and your true professionalism. It makes me feel respected and also shows your commitment to our team. I need everyone to follow the same policy!"

♥ "Connie, I notice you are really trying to get to the office on time! You are so open-minded and willing to improve. You're facing your biggest workplace challenge and succeeding in sticking to our punctuality policy! We need everyone to be on time."

♥ "Brenda, I know it has been hard for you to speak up and be assertive as a manager. I can see you are really trying to overcome this fear and get your supervisees to stay on task. You are getting better and better at it! Each manager is responsible for his or her team's performance."

♥ "Michael, I know it has been hard to keep yourself organized. I see that you are really trying…and your desk appears much neater! We appreciate your cooperation and team spirit, as your desk is the first one our clients see when they walk through the door! All desks are to be left in order."

Creative Recognition gives leaders even more control over the flow of energy in the workplace. Employees gain a sense that there is a new sheriff in town, and that the old paradigm of energy for negativity is being replaced with a positive flow of energy. Positivity neurons are firing in their minds, hearts, and spirits. In the spirit of Ken Blanchard's situational leadership teachings, we embrace the role of leader as coach. **Creative Recognition is one more tool that enables us to cultivate employees' willingness, interests and creativity by creating moments where success is inescapable—and then, we give the employee all of the credit for that success.**

Señora Corazon, chief executive officer of Creative Recognitions, Inc., inspires employees and managers by creatively recognizing as much success and compliance as possible. She is fearless and relentless, but she is also compassionate and nurturing.

Positivity Pulse Points: Creative Recognitions

✓ Watch for cues suggesting that employees are about to do exactly what they're supposed to, then make a request with which they're already on their way to complying. Voila! You've created a moment of success.

✓ When requests are complied with, give plentiful acknowledgment in the form of Experiential Recognition: what values or qualities is the employee upholding in his or her choices to comply with requests? Point out greatness qualities—character strengths and virtues.

✓ When not making requests, be as creative as possible in seeing opportunities to energize employees for their choices. Energize each increment the employee moves in the direction of success.

✓ If you have particularly challenging employees who are resistant to the flow of positive energy, offering Creative Recognitions frequently throughout the work day or shift can create a transcendental flow of success and positivity, breaking down resistance and opening hearts to a new and better way of relating.

At times, due to time constraints, lack of funding, budget cuts, stress, emergencies, and the like, we get caught up in what is *not* done versus what is already accomplished or is being accomplished in that moment. By focusing on and appreciating positive accomplishments instead of worrying about or dwelling on what isn't done, you energize that team member's desire to achieve. When a manager, frontline worker, or student's spirit is supported, he or she can thrive creatively, intellectually, emotionally, and socially, and this comes back to benefit everyone in the workplace.

The Nurtured Hearts Warriors team at Creative Recognitions, Inc., understood this well. They knew intuitively how to nurture hearts—and their commitment to doing so was held with warrior-like fierceness. Glasser speaks intensely to this point in his written work and seminars: the benefit of taking the warrior's path to nurturing hearts.

The Warrior's Way

One of the best modes for realizing what it means to be a peaceful warrior is the study of martial arts. My son, who was born in 1986, studied traditional Chitu-ryu karate when he was very young. The NHA's emphasis on warrior-like determination in remaining in the positive and refusing to give energy to negativity is echoed in the teachings of this school, where students learn that peace, perseverance and hard work—the peaceful warrior's way—are the ways to reach one's goals.

Its true essence is about being fearless in pursuit of one's goals—about courage, relentlessness, and achievement. The spiritual warrior is on a quest for self-knowledge and the ability to serve others with this knowledge. As the leader who brings the Positivity Pulse to your workplace, you are stepping onto the path of the spiritual warrior.

A warrior is much more than someone who learns to gain power over others through combat or warfare. The intense energy of warriorship can be used for peaceful purposes.

Chapter 6

The Truly Peaceful Workplace Begins with You

The word *peace* sometimes brings to mind its opposite: war and violence. The absence of these things, we think, is peace. But peace is more than the absence of violence: it is about harmony and balance. It is something to create proactively—not simply through attempts to eliminate conflict.

The words *shalom* (Hebrew) and *aloha* (Hawaiian) both translate to mean "peace," and they are used as greetings and farewells. In its depth, *shalom* conveys wishes for safety, good welfare, prosperity, security, fortune, and friendliness. On a personal level, it describes a nonviolent lifestyle that embraces respect, justice, and goodwill. All major religions and many cultural practices within tribal communities have teachings of peace.

Establishing a peaceful workplace requires focus on a "heart-set" and language of peace—cultivating peace in both our "inter" and "intra" styles of relating.

In industrialized countries we have, to some degree, lost the collective spirit of brotherhood and sisterhood prevalent in other countries—the spirit that understands the dynamic balance of true peace. I've found that the Nurtured Heart Approach is extremely helpful in navigating what, for some, may be a pretty steep learning curve into a more peaceful workplace.

When we create a space, any space—whether at home or in the workplace—that is one of peace, we are creating a space free from hostility and negativity. But we are also exploring opportunities to create new, healthy relationships and to heal existing relationships that have been afflicted by oppression and ignorance. This is achieved through compassionate communication—the kind of communication supported by the Nurtured Heart Approach.

Another Take on Compassionate Communication

> If you want others to be happy, practice compassion. If you want to be happy, practice compassion.
>
> —*The Dalai Lama*

> What I want in my life is compassion, a flow between myself and others based on a mutual giving from the heart.
>
> —*Marshall Rosenberg*

Marshall Rosenberg is internationally known as the creator of Nonviolent Communication, a series of methods that create true peace. These methods facilitate what Rosenberg calls *compassionate communication*.

NVC's definition of violence extends beyond attempts to physically harm others; it also includes the use of personal or systematic power to coerce others. This can be done through the language we use—particularly when that language threatens punishment or is designed to manipulate through guilt or a sense of obligation. According to NVC, even language that promises rewards in return for compliance as an attempt to control can be considered violent.

Nonviolent Communication involves empathically listening to the observations, feelings, needs, and requests of others, and honestly, clearly expressing your own observations, feelings, needs, and requests. Like the Nurtured Heart Approach, Nonviolent Communication is a shining example of the ways in which compassionate communication creates a foundation for peace. And both are languages that have to be learned and practiced.

Compassionate communication in general, and the Nurtured Heart Approach in particular, conveys the message: *You matter.* The recipient receives recognition simply by virtue of being. Whether you use the approach to consciously recognize a child in a classroom, a seasoned or new employee in a job, or yourself, you are promoting peace in your path.

Willingness to Be Acknowledged for Our Greatness: A Step toward Peace

Unfortunately, many of us resist being recognized for what we do right. Being recognized for the greatness inherent in our everyday actions can be a much bigger stretch. The same goes for adopting an approach to interacting with others that is consciously positive.

Upbringing plays a role. Most parenting emphasizes and energizes negativity, even so-called positive parenting. And for many of us conflict resolution and effective communication is learned in the context of problems and challenges, not as proactive ways of relating to others. Forms of communication that energize the positive are learned only as problem-solving tools. By the time we learn those techniques, most of us are hardwired to manage strong negative feelings through dysfunctional means of communicating. Most of us are working against a good deal of conditioning as we resolve to refuse to energize negativity.

In the bigger picture, the absence or loss of peace can be traced back to many social and cultural factors: political unrest, domination, oppression, economic inequalities, glass ceilings, racism, sexism, ageism, homophobia, and religious radicalism. How can our minds and hearts not be affected by these inherently violent, divisive political and social constructs? Until we become aware and committed to making that change that begins with each individual, we will fail to make a difference not only in these larger constructs, and in the workplace, but within our own lives.

In learning the Nurtured Heart Approach, we download new software to make this change. We learn techniques that enable us to practice speaking a language of nonviolence and positivity. Your major role in leadership is to be relentless and fearless with implementing this new style in your workplace. Keep resetting yourself into this new and healing way of relating. Set the example. People will get used to it—whether they like it or love it!

> *Returning to our hearts is such a simple concept that we may feel tempted to downplay its significance…but we mustn't, because a conscious return to our hearts frees the spirit and love and peace within us. And each of us—as well as the world as whole—is thirsting for the solace of living within the safety and serenity of love and peace.*
>
> –Sue Patton Thoele

In Glasser and Block's 2009 book *You Are Oprah: Igniting the Fires of Greatness,* the authors turned us on to what Glasser calls *greatness practice:* the use of the Nurtured Heart Approach on one's self to cultivate and expand into greatness. Greatness practice supports the reader in using the NHA to shine light on greatness in ourselves, family members, lovers, partners, spouses, and colleagues to build stronger, positive and deeper relationships. (If you aren't a fan of Oprah, don't be discouraged from the book or the greatness practice; Glasser uses her as an example of someone who lives the example of taking herself to the greatest heights—not only for her own gain, but in order to nurture greatness in others.)

Each person to whom I bring this approach comes closer to realizing that the power lies within him or her to make the change he or she wants to be. I might take credit for the knowledge and experience that I offer, but my main agenda is to get them to see the power and greatness that they hold and that I so clearly see. I often say, if one visit once per week with me changes people's lives, I'd be a great candidate for an interview with Oprah!

Conventional wisdom says we have to earn greatness. But greatness comes from within; it's a state of being. Most of us can fluently describe the greatness of others, but have a difficult time accepting and appreciating our own accomplishments. Let's begin within to ignite our own greatness.

To support yourself and others in standing in greatness, look no further than Glasser's "Top Eight to Being Great" as described by blogger and author Janice Taylor at *The Huffington Post:*

1. ***Accept It.*** Your greatness is inherent, inborn, a birthright of being human, a gift of the Creator. You are a unique expression of the Creator's greatness. Rejecting this self-evident truth doesn't negate it; but it negates your power to *express* your greatness. It takes a lot of energy to hide from the truth.

2. ***See It.*** Train yourself in the art of answering this question, "What's going right here?" Choose to see the things you think, say and do that are right,

the things that are going right. Choose to see the things that *could* be going wrong, but aren't. This is an art; and like all art forms, it requires practice and the ability to see things anew.

3. **Think It**: Choose to dwell, to linger, to consider everything that's right that you've diligently trained your new eyes to see. Rather than ruminating on your impatience, you choose to dwell on the split-second of patience prior to impatience. That's using your energetic power to expand your patience, to ignite your greatness.

4. **Appreciate It:** Choose to be grateful for the greatness and goodness that you are now able to see. Express your thankfulness. There are always deeper levels of gratefulness to explore. Prior to the Twin Towers falling, how much did you appreciate that they were standing?

5. **Feel It**: Emotions are so powerful that they sometimes scare us. So we try to stuff, deny, or outrun them. But feelings come from our hearts, and our hearts are the vehicle for transmitting greatness. The lie is that we have to act on our feelings. The truth is that we need only feel them. Feel them with every cell of your body, and you'll be tapping your life force.

6. **Do It:** When you accept your inherent greatness, and practice seeing it, thinking it and feeling it, there's no stopping you from manifesting greatness in your actions. You're the force of unstoppable greatness at home, at work, and in your relationships.

7. **Be It:** In consistently choosing the greatness practice, it eventually *becomes* you. You're no longer concerned about "doing it" or "doing it right," you simply *are*. It is an internal state of being that aligns spirit, soul, and body.

8. **Live It:** The final stage is self-transformation and co-creation. Your soul gets to fulfill itself and bring your greatness to the world as a manifestation of who you really are.

(http://www.huffingtonpost.com/janice-taylor/you-are-oprah-top-eight-t_b_209633.html; accessed July 20, 2010)

Greatness is an energy. The greatness practice is about the choices we make in every moment—small choices and large. We can go to greatness in every one of those choices. As you choose greatness, you'll discover a

Learning the Nurtured Heart Approach is like learning a new language, and like any new language, it takes practice and perseverance. It demands that we stop leaking our own negativity while holding a mindset that is governed by open-mindedness and openheartedness.

playground of godly qualities waiting for your conscious energizing in yourself and others.

In a sense, as leaders—whether we're classroom teachers, small business owners, religious leaders, or Fortune 500 CEOs—it is incumbent upon us to turn the tide of negativity in our workplaces. Moving into a peaceful, harmonious work environment starts within us as individuals.

I don't promise you that it will be easy; change is a challenge and people move in and out of change in varying ways. In such a workplace, employees' intensity and connection to their work can freely flow.

The *Flow* of the Nurtured Heart Workplace

In over forty years of research, psychologist Mihaly Csikszentmihalyi, a major contributor to the modern positive psychology movement, was able to identify and describe a state of being he called *flow*: optimal experience, where sense of time is lost and there is total engagement with the activity at hand. When leaders create an environment conducive to this kind of optimal experience, the rewards are manyfold: heightened creativity, better performance, an immense level of personal satisfaction.

Csikszentmihalyi, who was born in 1934, has gained wide recognition and best-selling-author status for his research into the nature of happiness and creativity. He is best known for his investigations into the concept of flow—a state he described to *Wired* magazine's John Geirland as "being completely involved in an activity for its own sake." By building positive relationships, inner wealth, and greatness in the workplace, we help to foster flow, which in turn fosters optimal performance.

> You're right in the work, you lose your sense of time, you're completely enraptured, you're completely caught up in what you're doing.... there's no future or past, it's just an extended present in which you're making meaning...
>
> —*Mark Strand*

In this state of flow, "[t]he ego falls away. Time flies. Every action, movement, and thought follows inevitably from the previous one, like playing jazz. Your whole being is involved, and you're using your skills to the utmost."

In Nurtured Heart terms, employees who are in a flow state can allow their intensity to take over in a way that makes them one with their work. By removing the restraint of negativity in a workplace rich in positive relationship, we allow a heightened level of performance—a smoother transition to a flow state where intensity blossoms.

Pause for a moment to hold this vision in your leader's heart. Breathe. Meditate on the magnificence of your workplace.

Take Action!

If you're committed to achieving the Positivity Pulse in your organization, begin with the following steps:

1. Create a sense of urgency.

There is some urgency to this call. In Kotter's work, this sense of exigency—as opposed to a more *laissez-faire* approach—is held up as key to making real changes happen. This has also been true in my experience. If you wish to create real change in your workplace, convey a sense that the moment for change is now.

2. Identify key players in your organizations who will attend the initial training.

Those leaders will then function as the Nurtured Heart Warriors in your organization.

3. Schedule your initial training.

Purchase reading materials for your entire staff. Require that your key players read these materials prior to the first training. Either enlist the help of a Nurtured Heart Advanced Trainer or plan to teach the approach yourself based on what you've learned here. See the resources section for information about purchasing books and hiring an Advanced Trainer.

4. Dust off that policy and procedures manual.

Determine what stays, what gets modified, and what goes. Be clear that you are setting clear rules and regulations, including consequences for noncompliance and rule violation.

5. Host the Positivity Pulse training.

Ignite the fire in your organization. Watch the transformation begin.

6. Monitor your outcomes.

Keep track of ways in which the approach is helping in your organization and how its application can be continually improved.

7. Adopt a warrior stance.

Maintain relentless, fearless warriorship around maintaining and increasing positivity in your organization.

8. Hold weekly mini-meetings to receive reports on your Positivity Pulse Project.

How is it transforming the workplace? How can it be better used for this purpose?

9. Hold monthly ongoing trainings for a period of six months following the initial training.

Ongoing coaching and training can be done via teleconference or in person and does not need to exceed one to two hours per event.

10. Stay creative and flexible.

Use your creativity to create continuous opportunities for your organization to grow into its greatness.

Hold to the Stands. Apply the techniques. Try the Positivity Pulse Action Steps described on the next page. Come up with your own Action Steps. Watch how your workplace transforms.

Remember the words you were told when this last adventure began, the words whispered quietly to your heart: Let the journey unfold. Let it be magical. The way has been prepared. People will be expecting you. Yes, you are being led.

—*Melody Beattie*

Positivity Pulse Action Steps

Once you have finished initial Nurtured Heart Approach training and identified the people in your organization who will be responsible for keeping the Positivity Pulse alive, try these action steps to keep that pulse moving and growing:

- Take a stand to *stop energizing negativity* from this day forward.

- Eliminate policies and procedures that energize negativity and modify, omit, or add new ones as necessary.

- Create clear rules, limits, and consequences.

- Consider creating a brief heart meditation to start the day. In only two or three minutes, you can get the workforce into their hearts before the day begins.

- Commit to energizing success in your workplace at every opportunity! Hang posters that will remind everyone in your workplace of the stands of the approach: try Shamu, the San Francisco Bay Bridge, or butterflies, or find other images that make sense in your workplace. Think visually, auditorily, kinesthetically, and experientially!

- Let your management team and every person in your organization know that they are expected to buy into the approach. Some people may be resistant, and that's OK, but you may decide that your workplace may not be a good fit for them. Others may have been waiting for this kind of shift, and they might surprise you with their enthusiasm!

- Establish your organization's core values. (Blanchard and Hodges would call these your organization's Ten Commandments.) Prioritize them. Gather feedback, but know that ultimately, as the leader, you get to decide what those values will look like. Post them and review with your entire organization.

- Identify your employees' signature strengths at www.authentichappiness.org. Watch how tapping into their strengths in their workplace leads them into a "flow" state in their work.

- Establish a Caring Hearts Wall of Fame where you publicly recognize achievements, service, and any other expression of greatness in your workplace.

- Send e-mails and texts that recognize positivity as you experience it, in real time. This is a great way to use modern technology! Don't wait. As the folks at Nike would say: Just do it!

- Reset e-mails and texts that have a negative tone or that cut into productivity time. Teach the reset back to greatness. Get on the phone or meet in person to work through conflict that is being energized in a negative way via texting and e-mailing. Negativity-energizing e-mails cut into productivity time and contribute to low morale. Some studies have shown that 80 percent of e-mail messages are misinterpreted.

- Identify a person responsible for collecting and disseminating Positivity News Blasts via e-mail on at least a monthly basis. Be sure this data is stored to determine eligibility criteria for Positivity Pulse awards at the end of the year.

A Final Story

As a consultant, I provide critical incident debriefings for major corporations. I had the privilege of being called in to support a group at Ricoh in New Jersey, where they were grieving the loss of a beloved manager who had climbed from the bottom rung of the ladder into a great leader.

The people gathered that day adored this manager not only for her brilliance as their leader but for her compassionate nature. When she traveled with someone who was Asian, she was concerned about the food they could find for dinner. When someone was juggling a full-time job and graduate school, she took the time to notice when the person seemed overwhelmed and cheered her on. When someone was upset about a project that did not seem to be running smoothly, she spoke to that person, expressing her feelings about his negative comments—but also intuitively resetting him back to their great relationship and to his greatness as a team player.

The stories shared that day revealed this leader's intelligence and compassion and all the ways in which these qualities influenced their workplace. I have never provided a debriefing where so many people came together as a collective—as a team. Their diversity was noticeable visually and auditorily, but the power in the love they shared for this woman could not have united them more. In that moment in time, they were one in *namaste*. I felt honored and blessed to be part of that circle. With tears in my eyes, feeling the power of that love, I thought, "Wow, I wish I had known this woman."

I humbly thank Gordan Marzano, Senior Manager, Human Resources at Ricoh Americas Corporation. He instinctively knew that to honor this woman's spirit in their workplace was to respect her team and her leadership style that which was of love and caring. As you can see she moved mountains in her department because she cared, honored and recognized those whom she served.

There's no greater call than that of helping others to create lasting, deep, mutually respectful relationships—to guiding them to that sense of *namaste*. In doing so, you have an incalculable, vast, and positive influence on the lives of others. I salute all of you who already lead with love. And for those of you ready to take this journey, I salute you too.

Resources

To get The Positivity Pulse in your workplace, contact Sherry A. Blair via e-mail at sherry@isisnj.us or by contacting her office at:

ISIS Innovative Specialists Inspirational Services, LLC
80 Park Street
Montclair, NJ 07042
Tel: 973-746-0333 Fax: 973-746-1533

References

Anderson, J. (2003). *The Transformation to Corporate Nirvana.* Salem, OR: Silver Falls Press.

Blanchard, K., Zigarmi, D. & Zigarmi, P. (1985). *Leadership and the One Minute Manager: Increasing Effectiveness Through Situational Leadership.* New York, NY: William Morrow and Company, Inc.

Blanchard, K. & Hodges, P. (2003). *The Servant Leader Transforming Your Heart, Head, Hands & Habits.* Nashville, TN: J. Countryman/Thomas Nelson, Inc.

Block, M. & Glasser, H. (2007). *All Children Flourishing Igniting the Greatness of Our Children.* Tucson, AZ: Nurtured Heart Publications.

Block, M. & Glasser, H. (2009). *You Are Oprah: Igniting the Fires of Greatness.* Tucson, AZ: Nurtured Heart Publications.

Easley, J. & Glasser, H. (1998). *Transforming the Difficult Child.* Tucson, AZ: Nurtured Heart Publications.

Freiberg, K. & Freiberg, J. (2005). *Guts: Companies That Blow The Doors Off Business-As-Usual.* New York, NY: Currency, Doubleday.

Glasser, H. & Block, M. (2010). *Notching Up the Nurtured Heart Approach: The Nurtured Heart Approach for Educators.* Tucson, AZ: Nurtured Heart Publications.

Kotter, J. P. (2008). *A Sense of Urgency.* Boston, MA: Harvard Business Press.

Peterson, C. & Seligman, S. (2004). *Character Strengths and Virtues: A Handbook and Classification.* Washington, DC: American Psychological Association.

Rosenberg, M. (2003). *Nonviolent Communication: A Language of Life.* Encinitas, CA: PuddleDancer Press.

Rosenberg, M. *Giving From the Heart: The Heart of Nonviolent Communication.* Retrieved from *Sentient Times,* Feb/Mar 2005, on October 23, 2010, 10:26 am.

Seligman, M. (2003). *Authentic Happiness: Using the New Positive Psychology to Realize Your Potential for Lasting Fulfillment.* New York, NY: The Free Press.

Johnson, S. (2002). *Who Moved My Cheese?* New York, NY: G.P. Putnam's Sons.

Wachs Book, E. (2001). *Why the Best Man for the Job Is a Woman: The Unique Female Qualities of Leadership.* New York, NY: Harper Business.

Wikipedia.com

About the Editor

Melissa Lynn Block is a freelance writer and editor. She has worked extensively with Howard Glasser, the developer of the Nurtured Heart Approach, as co-author and editor of books on the approach, and became an Advanced Trainer of the approach in 2008. She lives in Santa Barbara, California with her children, Sarah and Noah.

About the Author

As founder/CEO of her own company, Sherry Blair inspires and motivates others by applying and encouraging positivity. She uses her skills to teach others how to build effective teams, and use non-violent communication to achieve results and resolve conflict. Teaching others to speak from their hearts is a key constituent of the work she does.

She is a graduate of Rutgers University with a Bachelor of Arts in Psychology and Women's Studies. She went on to obtain her Master of Science in Social Work with a concentration in Policy Analysis and International Social Welfare as a graduate of Columbia University.

Additionally she is dually mastered in Industrial and Organizational Psychology. Sherry's areas of expertise are providing organizational consulting, coaching, behavioral health services, training and education. She assists organizations with performance enhancement, management coaching, team cohesiveness and effective communication.

Sherry is a New Jersey Licensed Clinical Social Worker, a Board Certified Professional Counselor and a Professional Coach. She is an Advanced Trainer/Certified Nurtured Heart Specialist currently serving on the Ethics & Global Summit 2011 Committees for Howard Glasser and The Nurtured Heart Approach, a transformational approach that changes lives.